P9-DVE-006

Flowers that are mostly blue   pg. 21

Flowers that are mostly green   pg. 51

Flowers that are mostly orange   pg. 55

Flowers that have prominent pink   pg. 75

Flowers that are mostly purple   pg. 127

Flowers that are mostly red   pg. 179

Flowers that are mostly white   pg. 207

Flowers that are mostly yellow   pg. 287

Wildflowers
of
Arizona
Field Guide

by Nora Mays Bowers,
Rick Bowers
and Stan Tekiela

ADVENTURE PUBLICATIONS
CAMBRIDGE, MINNESOTA

To my sister, Beth, for sharing her love of flowers with me - Nora

To Matt Johnson, who always kept plants on my mind and taught me so much about them - Rick

To my daughter, Abigail Rose, the sweetest flower in my life - Stan

Edited by Deborah Walsh

Cover, book and icon design by Jonathan Norberg

Photo credits by photographer and page number:
Cover photo: Desert Mariposa Lily by Nora Bowers
P. J. Alexander: 266 James M. André: 270 (fruit) Ralph Arvesen: 126 Larry
Blakely: 118 Kenneth L. Bowles: 284 Michael L. Charters: 182 (flower), 328
Christopher L. Christie: 246 (dried stems), 298 (both), 410 Audrey and George
DeLange: 38 George and Eve DeLange: 274 Dudley Edmondson: 256 Thomas
J. Elpel: 106 Golden State Images: 246 (flower) Lara Hartley Photography: 46
Richard Haug: 102 www.saguaro-juniper.com: 238 Hank Jorgensen: 308 (fruit)
T. Beth Kinsey: 44, 80, 86 (both), 240 (fruit), 260 (both), 282 (fruit), 286, 364,
366 Thomas Kornack: 342 (flower) Glen Lee: 236 Max Licher: 54 Don
Mammoser: 160, 212 (fruit), 334 Gary A. Monroe: 196 Gary A. Monroe/USDA-
NRCS Plants Database: 182 (plant), 208 Robert Potts/California Academy of
Sciences: 140 Larry Sansone: 166 Al Schneider: 134, 264, 270 (plant, flower)
David G. Schwaegler: 308 (flower) Stan Tekiela: 32, 34, 66 (both), 74, 116, 124
(both), 146, 148, 156, 158, 178, 186, 204, 212 (flower), 242, 258, 262, 268, 276
(both), 282 (flower), 336, 344, 376, 378, 386, 388 (fruit), 390, 396, 398, 402, 418
(both) Andy and Sally Wasowski/Lady Bird Johnson Wildflower Center: 198
Charles Webber/California Academy of Sciences: 358 www.shutterstock.com:
84 (inset) Kay Yatskievych: 210 Gena Zolotar: 84 (plant) Rick and Nora
Bowers: all other photos

10 9 8 7 6 5

Wildflowers of Arizona Field Guide
Copyright © 2008 by Nora Bowers, Rick Bowers and Stan Tekiela
Published by Adventure Publications
An imprint of AdventureKEEN
310 Garfield Street South
Cambridge, Minnesota 55008
(800) 678-7006
www.adventurepublications.net
All rights reserved
Printed in China
ISBN 978-1-59193-069-3 (pbk.)

TABLE OF CONTENTS

Introduction 6

Sample Page 19

The Wildflowers

    Blue 21

    Green 51

    Orange 55

    Pink 75

    Purple...127

    Red..179

    White 207

    Yellow...287

Glossary 420

Checklist/Index 425

About the Authors 430

ARIZONA AND WILDFLOWERS

Arizona is a great place for wildflower enthusiasts! From high mountains with cool pine forests and refreshing streams to the driest and hottest deserts, Arizona is fortunate to have an extremely diverse, often unique and a very healthy variety of wonderful wildflowers.

Wildflowers of Arizona Field Guide is an easy-to-use field guide to help the curious nature seeker identify 200 of the most common and widespread wildflowers in Arizona. It features, with a number of exceptions, the herbaceous wildflowers of Arizona. Herbaceous plants have green soft stems and die back to the ground each autumn. Some plants with woody stems have been included because these particular plants are very common and have large showy flowers. Since their bright colorful flowers are so noticeable, a sampling of the most common cacti has also been included.

Wildflowers of Arizona Field Guide is one in a series of five unique field guides for Arizona, including those for birds, mammals, trees and cacti.

STRATEGIES FOR IDENTIFYING WILDFLOWERS

Determining the color of the flower is the first step in a simple five-step process to identify a wildflower.

Because this field guide is organized by color, identifying an unknown wildflower is as simple as matching the color of the flower to the color section of the book. The color tabs on each page identify the color section.

The second step in determining the identity of a wildflower is the size. Is it a single flower or a cluster of flowers? Sometimes flowers are made up of many individual flowers in clusters that are perceived to be one larger flower. These are ordered by the size of the cluster, not the individual flower. Therefore, within each color section, the flowers are grouped with the single flowers first, followed by those with flower clusters. Each group is then arranged by size, from small to large. For example, a plant with a single small yellow flower will be in the beginning of the yellow section, while a large white flower cluster will be toward the end of the white section. The size may be shown as a range, with the average used to place the flower in size order. See page 432 for rulers to help estimate flower and leaf sizes.

Once you have determined the color and approximate size, observe the appearance of the flower. For the single flowers, note if the flower has a regular, irregular, bell or tube shape. If it is a cluster, is the general shape of the cluster flat, round or spike? Also, counting the number of petals might help to identify these individual flowers. Compare your findings with the descriptions on each page. Examining the flower as described should reduce identification possibilities of the wildflower to a few candidates.

The fourth step is to look at the leaves. There are several possible shapes or types of leaves. Simple leaves have only one leaf blade, but can be lobed. Compound leaves have a long central leafstalk with many smaller leaflets attached. Twice compound leaves have at least two leafstalks and many leaflets. Sometimes it is helpful to note if the leaves have an edge (margin) that is toothed or smooth, so look for this also. In cacti, the spines are actually modified leaves, so note their shape, number, length and color in each spine cluster.

For the fifth step, check how the leaf is attached to the stem. Some plants may look similar, but have different leaf attachments, so this can be very helpful. See if the leaves are attached opposite of each other along the stem, alternately, or whorled around a point on the stem. Sometimes the leaves occur at the base of the plant (basal). Some leaves do not have a leafstalk and clasp the stem at their base (clasping). In other cases, the stem appears to pass through the base of the leaf (perfoliate).

Using these five steps (color, size, shape, leaves and leaf attachment) will help you gather the clues needed to quickly and easily identify the common wildflowers of Arizona.

USING THE ICONS

Sometimes the botanical terms for leaf type, attachment and type of flower can be confusing and difficult to remember. Because of this, we have included icons at the bottom of each page. They can be used to quickly and visually match the main features of the plant to the specimen you are viewing without needing to completely understand the botanical terms. By using the photos, text descriptions and icons in this field guide, you should be able to quickly and easily identify most of the common wildflowers of Arizona.

The icons are arranged from left to right in the following order: flower cluster type, flower type, leaf type, leaf attachment and fruit. The first two flower icons refer to cluster type and flower type. While these are not botanically separate categories, we have made separate icons for them to simplify identification.

FLOWER CLUSTER ICONS

Flat

Round

Spike

(icon color is dependent on flower color)

Clusters (collections) of flowers can be categorized into one of three cluster types based on its overall shape. The flat, round and spike types refer to the cluster shape, which is easy to observe. Technically, there is another cluster type, composite, which appears as a single daisy-like flower, but is actually a cluster of many tiny flowers. Because this is often perceived as a flower type, we have included the icon in the flower type section. See page 9 for its description.

Some examples of cluster types

Flat

Round

Spike

FLOWER TYPE ICONS

     (icon color is dependent on flower color)

Regular　**Irregular**　**Composite**　**Bell**　**Tube**

Botanically speaking, there are many types of flowers, but in this guide, we are simplifying them to five basic types. Regular flowers are defined as having a round shape with three or more petals, lacking a disk-like center. Irregular flowers are not round, but uniquely shaped with fused petals. Bell flowers are hanging with fused petals. Tube flowers are longer and narrower than bell flowers and point up. Composite flowers (technically a flower cluster) are usually compact round clusters of tiny flowers appearing as one larger flower.

Some examples of flower types

Regular　　　　Irregular　　　　Bell

Tube　　　　Composite

disk flowers

ray flowers

Composite cluster: Although a composite flower is technically a type of flower cluster, we are including the icon in the flower type category, since most people unfamiliar with botany would see it as a separate flower type. A composite flower consists of petals (ray flowers) and/or a round disk-like center (disk flowers). Sometimes a flower has only ray flowers, sometimes only disk flowers, or both.

LEAF TYPE ICONS

Simple

Simple Lobed

Compound

Twice Compound

Palmate

Spines

Leaf type can be broken down into two main types: simple and compound. Simple leaves are leaves that are in one piece; the leaf is not divided into smaller leaflets. It can have teeth or be smooth along the edges. The simple leaf is depicted by the simple icon. Simple leaves may have lobes and sinuses that give the leaf a unique shape. These simple leaves with lobes are depicted by the simple lobed icon.

Some examples of leaf types

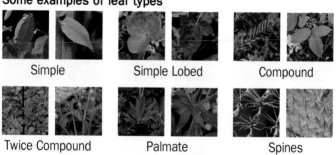

Simple

Simple Lobed

Compound

Twice Compound

Palmate

Spines

Compound leaves have two or more distinct small leaves, called leaflets, arising from a single stalk. In this book we are dividing compound leaves into regular compound, twice compound or palmate compound leaves. Twice compound leaves are those with many distinct leaflets that arise from a secondary leafstalk. Palmate compound leaves are those with three or more leaflets arising from a common central point. Cactus spines are depicted by the spine icon as a leaf type.

LEAF ATTACHMENT ICONS

Alternate   **Opposite**   **Whorl**   **Perfoliate**   **Clasping**   **Basal**

Leaves attach to the stems in different ways for different plants. Check to see where and how each leaf is attached to the main stem. There are six main types of attachment, as indicated, but sometimes a plant can have two different types of attachments. This is most often seen in the combination of basal leaves and leaves that attach along the main stem (cauline leaves), either alternate or opposite. These wildflowers have some leaves at the base of the plant, usually in a rosette pattern, and some leaves along the stem. In these cases, both icons are presented. For most plants there will only be one leaf attachment icon.

Some examples of leaf attachment

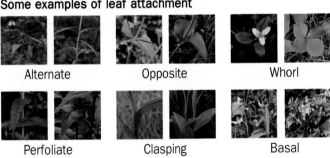

Alternate   Opposite   Whorl

Perfoliate   Clasping   Basal

Alternate leaves attach to the stem in an alternating pattern, while opposite leaves attach to the stem directly opposite from each other. Whorled leaves have three or more leaves that attach around the stem at the same point. Perfoliate leaves are also stalkless and have a leaf base that completely surrounds the main stem. Clasping leaves have no stalk and the base of the leaf partly surrounds the main stem. Basal leaves are those that originate at the base of a plant, near the ground, usually grouped in a round rosette.

FRUIT ICONS

  (icon color is dependent on fruit color at maturity)

Berry **Pod**

In some flower descriptions a fruit category has been included. This may be especially useful when a plant is not in bloom or when the fruit is particularly large or otherwise noteworthy. Botanically speaking, there are many types of fruit. We have simplified these often confusing fruit categories into two general groups, berry and pod.

Some examples of fruit types

Berry   Pod

The berry icon is used to depict a soft, fleshy, often round structure containing seeds. The pod icon is used to represent a dry structure that, when mature, splits open to release seeds.

MONTHS OF BLOOM

Most wildflowers have a specific season of blooming. You probably won't see, for example, the spring-blooming Desert Mariposa Lily blooming in summer or fall. In the lower deserts of Arizona, spring (February) and summer (beginning of May) come earlier than and fall (late October) comes later than it does in the higher mountains and in most of the rest of the United States, so we have specified the months, rather than the seasons, during which a wildflower blooms. Knowing the months of bloom can help you narrow your selection as you try to identify an unknown flower.

LIFE CYCLE/ORIGIN

The life cycle of a wildflower describes how long a wildflower lives. Annual wildflowers are short-lived. They sprout, grow and bloom in only one season, never to return except from seed. Most wildflowers have perennial life cycles that last many years. Perennial wildflowers are usually deeply rooted plants that grow from the roots each year. They return each year from their roots, but they also produce seeds to start other perennial plants. Similar to the annual life cycle is the biennial life cycle. This group of plants takes two seasons of growth to bloom. In the first year, the plant produces a low growth of basal leaves. During the second year, the plant sends up a flower stalk from which it produces seeds for starting new plants. However, the original plant will not return for a third year of growth.

Origin indicates whether the plants are native or non-native. Most of the wildflowers in this book originate in Arizona and are considered native plants. Non-native plants were often introduced unintentionally when they escaped from gardens or farms. All of the non-native plants in this book are now naturalized in Arizona.

LIFE ZONES/HABITATS

Sometimes noting the habitat surrounding a flower in question can be a clue to its identity. In Arizona, ecologists define nine distinct life zones, but for simplicity in this book, only seven will be considered. These life zones have characteristic plant and animal species based on temperature differences found at various elevations combined with yearly rainfall. The elevation range of a life zone is related to how far north or south in Arizona the zone occurs and how much rain the zone receives, thus the elevational ranges may overlap. Some plants are only found in certain life zones; others are generalists and can be found in more than one zone or even in all seven.

Desert scrub habitats range from 100-6,500 feet (30-1,980 m), but more importantly, this life zone is defined by rainfall of 12 inches (30 cm) or less per year. The dominant variety of shrubs of this zone is dependent upon the zone's location in Arizona and the type of desert in which the zone occurs. It is unique due to the presence of a wide variety of cacti, from the giant saguaro, which can be as tall as a power pole, to tiny pincushion cacti. Many of the wildflowers in this book, such as California Poppy, Arroyo Lupine or Owl's Clover, are short-lived annuals (ephemerals) that only grow and bloom in the deserts after good winter rains.

At some elevations, the **grasslands** life zone mixes with or replaces desert scrub habitats. Grasslands range from 3,000-7,000 feet (915-2,135 m) and have rainfall averages of 17 inches (43 cm) or less per year. Pure grasslands contain mostly shrubless stands of grasses, with some scattered evergreen oaks and mesquite trees. This zone suffers from overgrazing by cattle and the introduction of exotic grasses. New Mexico Thistles are common along roads in this life zone during spring and Summer Poppies bloom over large areas following the summer rains.

Running roughly east to west in a broken band just south of the rim of the Grand Canyon lies the **interior chaparral** life zone.

ranges from 3,000-8,000 feet (915-2,440 m) and has an annual rainfall of 15-25 inches (38-64 cm). Interior chaparral consists of a unique, dense community of deep-rooted evergreen shrubs and trees that have adapted to a habitat defined by frequent fires and that can easily regrow following fire. Palmer Penstemons, Blackfoot Daisies, and Dogweed are typical wildflowers found in this life zone.

Oak/pinyon pine/juniper woodlands occur at elevations between 4,000-7,000 feet (1,220-2,135 m) with yearly rainfall averaging 12-24 inches (30-61 cm). Sometimes this habitat overlaps with the grasslands, with grasses growing beneath widely spaced trees. In northern Arizona, this zone includes several species of evergreen juniper trees, as well as pinyon pines. Evergreen oaks mixed with pinyon pines are predominant in this zone in southern Arizona, where the bright lavender wildflower, Dakota Mock Vervain, is often found growing beneath oaks.

The **riparian deciduous** life zone lies within all the other life zones, but only near streams or dry streambeds with intermittently running surface water (washes). In soils around dry washes, underground streams supplement the moisture supplied by sporadic rain or snow, providing water to deep-rooted plants. Columbines, larkspurs and monkeyflowers are some of the wildflowers commonly found in riparian soils. However, moisture-loving, usually riparian plants can be found far from streams at higher and cooler elevations, where more rain falls and evaporative water loss is reduced. During drought, desert-adapted wildflower species, such as lupines and fleabane, also concentrate near streams and washes. Most plants seen in areas around streams are larger than usual due to the increased moisture in the soil. "Riparian," from the Latin *riparus*, means "bank" and refers to the land adjoining streams, while "deciduous" applies to the many tree species in this zone that shed their leaves in autumn.

COMMON NAME
Scientific name

Color indicator

Family: common family name (scientific family name)

Height: average range of mature plant

Flower: general description, may include cluster type, type of flower, color, size, number of petals or description of flower stem

Leaf/Spines: general description, may include shape, size, color, lobes, leaflets, teeth, veins, attachment, leafstalk or description of plant stem

Fruit: berry or pod, may include shape, color or size

Bloom: range of months when flower blooms

Cycle/Origin: annual, perennial, biennial; native or non-native

Zone/Habitat: zones such as desert scrub, grasslands, interior chaparral, oak/pinyon pine/juniper woodlands, riparian deciduous, montane or subalpine and elevation ranges; places found, may include soil types

Range: throughout or part of Arizona where found

Notes: Helpful identification information, history, origin and other interesting gee-whiz nature facts.

Not all icons are found on every page.
See preceding pages for icon descriptions.

CLUSTER TYPE	FLOWER TYPE	LEAF TYPE	LEAF ATTACHMENT	FRUIT
Spike	**Regular**	**Simple**	**Alternate**	**Berry**

MINIATURE WOOLLY STAR
Eriastrum diffusum

Family: Phlox (Polemoniaceae)

Height: 1-8" (2.5-20 cm)

Flower: tubular star-shaped flower, ½" (1 cm) wide, is blue to lavender to whitish, has 5 fused petals spreading into pointed lobes around a yellow center; held by 5 woolly, whitish green sepals; loosely grouped flowers are backed by woolly, dark green bracts

Leaf: narrowly lance-shaped leaves, ½-1" (1-2.5 cm) long, are smooth or woolly above with smooth or lobed margins; fluffy wool at leaf attachments (axis); white-haired, reddish brown stems

Bloom: Mar-Jun

Cycle/Origin: annual; native

Zone/Habitat: desert scrub and grasslands at 1,000-5,000' (305-1,525 m); flats, along washes, playas, mesas

Range: throughout

Notes: The genus name *Eriastrum* is from the Greek word *erion* for "wool" and *astrum* for "star," meaning that the plants are "woolly with star-like flowers." After heavy winter rains, this beautiful little flower can carpet large areas of deserts in Arizona. The seeds can be purchased from nurseries for cultivation. The only other *Eriastrum* in Arizona, the very similar Desert Woolly Star (*E. eremicum*) (not shown), occurs in the western two-thirds of Arizona, has slightly larger flowers with 2-6 lobes and has fewer, narrower leaves.

FLOWER
TYPE

LEAF TYPE

LEAF
ATTACHMENT

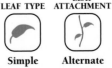

Tube

Simple

Alternate

FRANCISCAN BLUEBELLS
Mertensia franciscana

Family: Forget-me-not (Boraginaceae)

Height: 12-36" (30-91 cm)

Flower: groups of drooping, light blue-to-dark blue flowers; each slender bell-shaped flower, ⅝" (1.5 cm) long, has 5 rounded lobes; can be purplish blue to pink or white

Leaf: lance-shaped, dark green leaves, 1-5" (2.5-13 cm) long, fuzzy above with prominent veins and pointed tips; alternate, but pairs of leaves at the end of stems are opposite; leaves turn red or purple in autumn

Bloom: Jun-Sep

Cycle/Origin: perennial; native

Zone/Habitat: montane and subalpine at 6,000-11,500' (1,830-3,510 m); under ponderosa pines or fir trees, along streams

Range: northeastern and southeastern corners of Arizona

Notes: This tall plant is common along streams, in moist meadows and in forest clearings. It grows as a single plant, in small groups or in large dense colonies with hundreds of blooms. Franciscan Bluebells can be found on the San Francisco Peaks, the tallest mountains in Arizona. These peaks ring a dormant volcano and are sacred to Navajo, Hopi and Havasupai Indians. Species name *franciscana* is for these mountains, which were named in honor of the Catholic saint, St. Francis.

FLOWER TYPE	LEAF TYPE	LEAF ATTACHMENT
Bell	Simple	Alternate

ARIZONA MORNING GLORY
Evolvulus arizonicus

Family: Morning Glory (Convolvulaceae)

Height: 1-4' (30-122 cm)

Flower: flat, round, sky blue-to-purplish blue (sometimes white) flower, ¾" (2 cm) wide, has 10 fused petals and sepals surrounding a star-shaped white center

Leaf: narrowly lance-shaped, grayish green leaves, ½-1" (1-2.5 cm) long, with fuzzy short white hairs; thread-like sprawling stem

Bloom: Apr-Oct

Cycle/Origin: perennial; native

Zone/Habitat: desert scrub and grasslands at 2,200-5,000' (670-1,525 m); along washes, roadsides, slopes, flats

Range: scattered locations throughout Arizona, but mainly in a band from the northwestern to the southeastern corners, covering two-thirds of the state

Notes: A stunningly beautiful, commonly seen wildflower of the deserts, the flowers and stems appear too delicate to grow in such a harsh environment. The slightest touch bruises the flower, yet the slim stem sprawls along the ground or climbs the nearest plant or rock for support, as if not bothered by the arid heat. Also called Arizona Blue Eyes for the flower's round shape and blue color of a human eye. Similar to the non-native Slender Morning Glory (*E. alsinoides*) (not shown), which also occurs in southern Arizona, has compound leaves with round leaflets and has smaller flowers.

FLOWER TYPE	LEAF TYPE	LEAF ATTACHMENT
Regular	Simple	Alternate

BIRD'S BILL DAYFLOWER
Commelina dianthifolia

Family: Spiderwort (Commelinaceae)

Height: 6-15" (15-38 cm)

Flower: intensely blue flowers, 1" (2.5 cm) wide, with 3 triangular petals and yellow-tipped flower parts; each bloom is held in a large, folded, boat-shaped green bract

Leaf: narrow grass-like blades, 2-6" (5-15 cm) long, alternating along and clasping the stem

Bloom: Jul-Sep

Cycle/Origin: perennial; native

Zone/Habitat: oak/pinyon pine/juniper woodlands, montane, subalpine at 4,000-9,500' (1,220-2,895 m); clearings among pines or other conifers, meadows

Range: eastern three-quarters of Arizona

Notes: Called "Dayflower" for the flower's habit of opening early in the morning and wilting by noon. This showy wildflower is most commonly seen among ponderosa pines and is easily found in late summer blooming on Mount Lemmon in the Santa Catalina Mountains, just north of Tucson. Often cultivated for its unusual blue flowers, it can be grown from seed and blooms in the first year. A good plant for rock gardens, containers and borders. Hardy in temperatures down to 18°F (-8°C), but needs extra water in arid areas in the West.

FLOWER TYPE	LEAF TYPE	LEAF ATTACHMENT	LEAF ATTACHMENT
Regular	Simple	Alternate	Clasping

IVYLEAF MORNING GLORY
Ipomoea hederacea

Family: Morning Glory (Convolvulaceae)

Height: 3-9' (.9-2.7 m); vine

Flower: trumpet-shaped blue flowers, 1-2" (2.5-5 cm) wide, have fused petals flaring widely around a white center and a sharp tip where petals join; bloom held by a long pointed hairy calyx; 1-3 flowers per stalk

Leaf: hairy, long-stalked, ivy-like leaves, 1-6" (2.5-6 cm) long and equally as wide, are overall heart-shaped and usually divided into 3-5 broad pointed lobes

Bloom: Jul-Nov

Cycle/Origin: annual; non-native

Zone/Habitat: desert scrub, grasslands, oak/pinyon pine/juniper woodlands and riparian deciduous at 1,000-5,500' (305-1,675 m); along washes, disturbed soils, along roads and railroads

Range: southernmost quarter of Arizona and the north central part of the state

Notes: A tropical plant native to Central and South America that has naturalized in the U.S., escaping from gardens. Reaches its farthest west range in Arizona, extending east throughout the country. Can be a nuisance weed in agricultural fields. The large and gaudy flowers can be purple, white or pink, and the hairy stem trails or climbs on trees or shrubs. Blossoms open only for one day, then wilt. When the vine is vigorously shaken, the blooms begin to close.

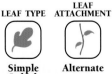

FLOWER TYPE	LEAF TYPE	LEAF ATTACHMENT
Tube	Simple Lobed	Alternate

LONG-FLOWERED GILIA
Ipomopsis longiflora

Family: Phlox (Polemoniaceae)

Height: 4-24" (10-61 cm)

Flower: star-shaped, tubular, whitish blue flower, 1-2" (2.5-5 cm) long; petals are fused into a narrow long reddish tube and spread into 5 pointed lobes veined with purple; flower has a white center

Leaf: thread-like stem leaves, ½-2½" (1-6 cm) long, are bright green; lower leaves are divided into lobes; basal leaves wither before the plant flowers

Fruit: oval green capsule, turning brown, ⅓" (.8 cm) long

Bloom: May-Nov, after rainfall

Cycle/Origin: annual, biennial; native

Zone/Habitat: all life zones except riparian deciduous at 2,000-9,500' (610-2,745 m); canyons, limestone soils

Range: throughout, except the southwestern corner

Notes: One of 14 species of *Ipomopsis* in Arizona. Long-flowered Gilia is very common near Greer and Springerville in northeastern Arizona, occurring along roads in thick groups of 50-60 plants. Also called Blue Gilia or Blue Starflower for the overall bluish appearance of the purple-veined petals. The light color of the slender flowers, the thin stems and thread-like leaves make this plant hard to spot and make it appear too fragile for the harsh desert habitat, where it can also be found.

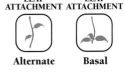

FLOWER TYPE	LEAF TYPE	LEAF ATTACHMENT	LEAF ATTACHMENT	FRUIT
Tube	Simple Lobed	Alternate	Basal	Pod

PRAIRIE SPIDERWORT
Tradescantia occidentalis

Family: Spiderwort (Commelinaceae)

Height: 10-30" (25-76 cm)

Flower: cluster of up to 10 flowers, each 1-2" (2.5-5 cm) wide, with 3 violet blue petals surrounding a golden yellow center; flowers open only a few at a time and are sometimes pink to white

Leaf: grass-like, arching, bluish green leaves, 6-15" (15-37.5 cm) long, clasp the stem at the base; each leaf has long parallel veining and is folded lengthwise, forming a V-groove

Bloom: Apr-Sep

Cycle/Origin: perennial; native

Zone/Habitat: grasslands, oak/pinyon pine/juniper woods, montane at 3,000-7,000' (915-2,135 m); along roads

Range: throughout, except the northwestern corner

Notes: Unusual-looking plant with exotic-looking flowers. Flowers open in the morning and often wilt by noon on hot days. "Spider" comes from several characteristics unique to the plant. One is the angular leaf attachment, suggestive of the legs of a sitting spider; another is the stringy, mucilaginous sap that strings out like a spider's web when the leaf is torn apart. "Wort" is derived from *wyrt*, an Old English word for "plant." Flowers change from blue to purple when exposed to air pollution, thus it has recently been used as a natural barometer for air quality.

FLOWER TYPE	LEAF TYPE	LEAF ATTACHMENT	LEAF ATTACHMENT
Regular	Simple	Alternate	Clasping

WESTERN BLUE FLAX
Linum lewisii

Family: Flax (Linaceae)

Height: 12-36" (30-91 cm)

Flower: sky blue-to-lavender flowers, 1-2" (2.5-5 cm) wide, have 5 broad fan-shaped petals around a greenish center; blossoms last only 1 day

Leaf: narrowly lance-shaped or thread-like, bluish green leaves, ½-1" (1-2.5 cm) long, with sharply pointed tips, mostly alternate, some opposite or whorled; stems densely leafy

Bloom: Apr-Nov, flowers profusely over 6 weeks

Cycle/Origin: perennial; native

Zone/Habitat: grasslands, oak/pinyon pine/juniper woodlands and montane at 3,200-9,000' (975-2,745 m); among ponderosa pines, disturbed rocky ground

Range: northern half of Arizona, scattered in the southern half of the state

Notes: *Linum* is from an old Greek name for "flax" and *lewisii* is for Meriwether Lewis of the Lewis and Clark Expedition, who explored the American West in the early 1800s, covering nearly 8,000 miles (12,880 km) by boat, horseback and on foot. Although not a botanist, he and Clark brought back this pretty, blue wildflower and many other plant species new to science. Widespread throughout the West and Midwest. Sometimes called Prairie Flax, its flowers can be white.

FLOWER TYPE	LEAF TYPE	LEAF ATTACHMENT	LEAF ATTACHMENT	LEAF ATTACHMENT
Regular	Simple	Alternate	Opposite	Whorl

CHIA
Salvia columbariae

Family: Mint (Lamiaceae)

Height: 4-20" (10-50 cm)

Flower: round cluster, 1-2" (2.5-5 cm) wide, of tiny neon blue-to-pale blue flowers with spine-tipped maroon bracts below; sometimes 1 cluster at top of stem, often 2-4 clusters surround the stem at intervals; flowers have a skunk-like odor

Leaf: oblong basal leaves, 1-4" (2.5-10 cm) long, are thick, wrinkled, sticky, with deep irregular rounded lobes, tiny grayish bristles above; few smaller stem leaves found only on lowest part of square stem

Bloom: Mar-May

Cycle/Origin: annual; native

Zone/Habitat: desert scrub, grasslands interior chaparral below 3,500' (1,065 m); slopes, dry disturbed soils

Range: two-thirds of Arizona, in a wide band from the northwestern to southeastern corners of the state

Notes: Historically, American Indians cultivated this plant along with corn; large plots of Chia still flower where their ancient villages once stood. They ate the nutritious nut-flavored seeds and drank a minty beverage of ground seeds mixed with water. The tiny nutlets were soaked in water to make a sticky poultice used to treat fevers and wounds. Chia is a traditional food useful in treating diabetes, a disease common among modern-day American Indian tribes.

CLUSTER TYPE	FLOWER TYPE	LEAF TYPE	LEAF ATTACHMENT	LEAF ATTACHMENT

Round	Irregular	Simple Lobed	Opposite	Basal

BAJADA LUPINE
Lupinus concinnus

Family: Pea or Bean (Fabaceae)

Height: 4-12" (10-30 cm)

Flower: dense violet-blue spike, 1-3½" (2.5-9 cm) long, has pea-like flowers, ¼-½" (.6-1 cm) long, in a spiral; each bloom has an upper petal (banner) spotted with yellowish white; lower petal (keel) is faintly streaked darker blue; several spikes per plant

Leaf: round, densely hairy, grayish green basal leaves, 1-1½" (2.5-4 cm) wide, divided into 5-9 narrow oval leaflets; leaves on hairy, sprawling or erect stems

Fruit: hairy tan seedpod, ⅝" (1.5 cm) long, has 3-5 seeds

Bloom: Mar-May

Cycle/Origin: annual; native

Zone/Habitat: desert scrub below 5,000' (1,525 m); lower mountain slopes (bajadas), burned areas, sandy soils

Range: throughout, except the southwestern corner

Notes: "Bajada" is Spanish for "slope," where these low-growing hairy plants are often found, and refers to fan-shaped debris deposited by floodwaters rushing out of a mountain canyon. Common in sandy soils throughout the Southwest, from southern California to western Texas and south into Mexico. In springtimes following heavy winter rains, it lines the roadsides of the Pinal Pioneer Parkway from Tucson to Florence, Arizona. *Concinnus* means elegant, thus this species is also called Elegant Lupine.

CLUSTER TYPE	FLOWER TYPE	LEAF TYPE	LEAF ATTACHMENT	FRUIT
Spike	Irregular	Palmate	Basal	Pod

BLUE BONNET LUPINE
Lupinus palmeri

Family: Pea or Bean (Fabaceae)

Height: 13-16" (33-40 cm)

Flower: cylindrical dense spike, 3-4½" (7.5-11 cm) long, of many pea-like, blue-to-purple flowers; each flower, ⅓" (.8 cm) long, appears to have 3 petals, but actually has 5 petals fused together

Leaf: each hand-shaped leaf, 2½" (6 cm) wide, has 5-8 slender pointed oval leaflets; leaves on long, velvety, grayish green stems rising mostly from the base

Fruit: pea-like green pod, turning tan, ¾" (2 cm) long, is oval and flat, covered with short fuzzy hairs

Bloom: Apr-Oct

Cycle/Origin: perennial; native

Zone/Habitat: montane at 6,000-8,000' (1,830-2,440 m); under ponderosa pines

Range: throughout, except the southwestern corner

Notes: This tall, showy species is the most common lupine in the ponderosa pine forests of the montane life zone. The spike cluster blooms from the bottom up, with the newer flowers a light blue and older flowers turning a deep blue. The leaflets are grayish green and outlined with a smooth gray margin. Lupines are able to grow in poor or disturbed soils since they have the ability to fix nitrogen from the air, which adds to the fertility of the soil.

CLUSTER TYPE	FLOWER TYPE	LEAF TYPE	LEAF ATTACHMENT	LEAF ATTACHMENT	FRUIT
	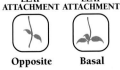				
Spike	Irregular	Palmate	Opposite	Basal	Pod

ARROYO LUPINE
Lupinus sparsiflorus

Family: Pea or Bean (Fabaceae)

Height: 8-16" (20-40 cm)

Flower: sparse spike cluster, 6-8" (15-20 cm) long, of pea-like blue flowers, each ½" (1 cm) long; upper petal (standard) has a yellow spot, lower petals (keel) have darker blue streaks and are hairy below

Leaf: each leaf has 5-11 narrow pointed leaflets arranged in a finger-like spread; leaves are 1-1½" (2.5-4 cm) wide, on stems rising mostly from the base

Fruit: green seedpod, turning beige, 1½" (4 cm) long, grows horizontally from the spike

Bloom: Jan-May

Cycle/Origin: annual; native

Zone/Habitat: desert scrub, grasslands at 100-3,000' (30-915 m); flats, lower mountain slopes (bajadas), mesas

Range: two-thirds of Arizona, in a wide band from the northwestern to southeastern parts of the state

Notes: "Arroyo" is Spanish for "creek," referring to a dry streambed (wash) through which water flows intermittently, along which this plant is often found. In years with good winter rains, Arroyo Lupine has some of the desert's most conspicuous blooms. Like all lupines, the leaflets turn to face the sun throughout the day, maximizing the amount of sunlight the plant absorbs.

CLUSTER TYPE	FLOWER TYPE	LEAF TYPE	LEAF ATTACHMENT	LEAF ATTACHMENT	FRUIT
			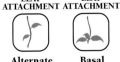		
Spike	Irregular	Palmate	Alternate	Basal	Pod

BARESTEM LARKSPUR
Delphinium scaposum

Family: Buttercup (Ranunculaceae)

Height: 10-24" (25-61 cm)

Flower: open loose spike, 5-12" (13-30 cm) long, of sky blue-to-royal blue flowers, 1" (2.5 cm) wide; each bloom has 5 blue sepals (upper sepal with long backward-curving purple spur) and 3 smaller blue petals (erect fourth petal is white)

Leaf: mostly basal, long-stalked leaves, are shaped like a half circle, ½-2½" (1-6 cm) wide, with flat bases and and deeply divided into 5 irregular-toothed lobes

Fruit: narrow brown seedpod, ½" (1 cm) long, 3-parted

Bloom: Feb-May

Cycle/Origin: perennial; native

Zone/Habitat: desert scrub, grasslands, oak/pinyon pine/juniper woodlands below 5,000' (1,525 m); mesas, hills

Range: throughout Arizona, except the southwestern and southeastern corners

Notes: *Scaposum*, Latin for "stem" or "scape," is for the nearly leafless flower stalk. Flowers at the bottom of the spike open first. In spring, hike King's Canyon Trail in the Tucson Mountains, north of the famous Arizona-Sonoran Desert Museum, to see this spectacular wildflower. Parts of the plant were made into a wash, which was used by Navajo or Hopi Indian mothers following childbirth.

CLUSTER TYPE	FLOWER TYPE	LEAF TYPE	LEAF ATTACHMENT	FRUIT
Spike	Irregular	Simple Lobed	Basal	Pod

DESERT LARKSPUR
Delphinium parishii

Family: Buttercup (Ranunculaceae)

Height: 7-24" (18-61 cm)

Flower: open loose spike, 5-16" (13-40 cm) long, with scattered sky blue-to-dark lavender flowers, 1" (2.5 cm) wide; blooms have 5 petal-like pointed sepals (upper sepal with a long backward-curving purple spur) and 4 smaller hairy petals

Leaf: grayish green leaves, ½-3" (1-7.5 cm) wide, deeply divided into irregular narrow pointed lobes and growing on long stalks from lower third or base of stem; most leaves wither by the time plant blooms

Fruit: narrow long brown seedpod, ¾" (2 cm) long

Bloom: Feb-Jun

Cycle/Origin: perennial; native

Zone/Habitat: desert scrub below 5,000' (1,525 m); arroyos

Range: south central and northwestern Arizona, combined to include about half of the state

Notes: The most drought-tolerant larkspur in the United States, with the size and number of leaves varying according to climate. It can be found along washes in the Silverbell Mountains in Ironwood Forest National Monument, west of Tucson. All the plant parts contain poisonous alkaloids and should never be eaten or even handled by people. Fatal to livestock if consumed in large amounts.

CLUSTER TYPE	FLOWER TYPE	LEAF TYPE	LEAF ATTACHMENT	LEAF ATTACHMENT	FRUIT

Spike	Irregular	Simple Lobed	Alternate	Basal	Pod

COLUMBIAN MONKSHOOD
Aconitum columbianum

Family: Buttercup (Ranunculaceae)

Height: 1-7' (.3-21 m)

Flower: very open spike clusters, 6-22" (15-56 cm) long, of dark blue-to-velvet purple flowers, 1" (2.5 cm) long; blooms have 5 petal-like sepals with the uppermost forming a high arching "hood," 2 backward-curving side "wings" and 2 forming the split bottom lip; center of green flower parts

Leaf: wide, hand-shaped, dark green leaves, 1-7" (2.5-18 cm) wide, have 3-5 deep, wedge-shaped lobes with toothed or jaggedly lobed edges; hollow stem

Fruit: vase-shaped pods, ½" (1 cm) long, have black seeds

Bloom: Jun-Sep

Cycle/Origin: perennial; native

Zone/Habitat: riparian deciduous, montane, subalpine at 5,000-10,000' (1,525-3,050 m); along mountain streams

Range: northern half and southeastern corner of Arizona

Notes: The foliage is frequently hidden, with only the spike of blue flowers rising above other vegetation. Usually grows as tall as 3 feet (.9 m), but can grow taller. Found throughout the West and as far north as Alaska; in Arizona, it is limited to the cooler mountains, wherever moist soils are present. *Aconitum* means "unconquerable poison." Most species in the genus are, in fact, extremely poisonous.

CLUSTER TYPE

Spike

FLOWER TYPE

Irregular

LEAF TYPE

Simple Lobed

LEAF ATTACHMENT

Alternate

FRUIT

Pod

CANAIGRE DOCK
Rumex hymenosepalus

Family: Buckwheat (Polygonaceae)

Height: 2-4' (61-122 cm)

Flower: dense spike cluster, 12" (30 cm) long, is pointed at the tip and widest in the middle; cluster made up of many tiny, pinkish green flowers; each flower has heart-shaped sepals and petals

Leaf: basal leaves, 3-12" (7.5-30 cm) long, are arching, tongue-shaped and have long stout succulent stalks

Fruit: 3-sided, heart-shaped winged capsule, ⅓" (.8 cm) long, is green, turning red at maturity

Bloom: middle Feb-Apr at lower elevations, until June at medium elevations

Cycle/Origin: perennial; native

Zone/Habitat: desert scrub, grasslands, riparian deciduous, 1,000-6,000' (305-1,830 m); fallow fields, alkaline soils

Range: throughout Arizona, except the southwestern and southeastern corners of the state

Notes: The very large basal leaves produced in the spring were historically cooked as greens, thus its other common name, Wild Rhubarb. It sends up a stout, conspicuous flower stalk covered with tiny pinkish green flowers, which are followed by showy, heart-shaped seed capsules that turn pink or red when mature. Canaigre Dock contains large amounts of tannin, which is useful in making leather products. Also called Tanner's Dock.

CLUSTER TYPE	FLOWER TYPE	LEAF TYPE	LEAF ATTACHMENT	FRUIT
Spike	**Irregular**	**Simple**	**Basal**	**Pod**

ELKWEED
Frasera speciosa

Family: Gentian (Gentianaceae)

Height: 2-6' (.6-1.8 m)

Flower: tall, cylindrical, whitish green spikes, 2-6' (.6-1.8 m) long, made up of densely packed, star-shaped flowers; each bloom, 1½" (4 cm) wide, has 4 greenish (flecked with purple) petals with fringed glands

Leaf: long oval basal leaves, 6-12" (15-30 cm) long, fuzzy below, thick with smooth edges; stalk has many leaves in whorls of 4-6, upper leaves smaller

Bloom: May-Aug

Cycle/Origin: perennial; native

Zone/Habitat: all life zones except desert scrub at 5,000-10,000' (1,525-3,050 m); among conifers or aspens, along roads, sunny grassy hillsides, rocky slopes, rich soils

Range: northern half and southeastern corner of Arizona

Notes: Sometimes called Deer Ears for the long oval leaves, this is one of the most conspicuous and common mountain plants. The species name *speciosa* means "showy" and refers to its tall stout flower spikes, thus another name, Monument Plant. Colonies of these plants flower all at the same time, but only every few years. Each Elkweed has a very large basal rosette of leaves for most of its lifetime of 20-80 years and sends up the large flowering spike only once, then dies. The decaying, fallen flowering stalk then provides shelter and nutrition for its own seedlings, enabling them to survive.

CLUSTER TYPE	FLOWER TYPE	LEAF TYPE	LEAF ATTACHMENT	LEAF ATTACHMENT
Spike	Regular	Simple	Whorl	Basal

ARIZONA HONEYSUCKLE
Lonicera arizonica

Family: Honeysuckle (Caprifoliaceae)

Height: 3-18' (.9-5.5 m); vine

Flower: groups of 3-12 tubular orange flowers tip the stem; each bloom, 1-1½" (2.5-4 cm) long, has a narrow yellow throat and barely protruding flower parts

Leaf: oval, sticky, finely hairy, bluish green leaves, 2-3" (5-7.5 cm) long; 1 to several stalkless pairs of upper leaves are joined at their bases

Fruit: clusters of oval shiny red berries

Bloom: Jun-Jul

Cycle/Origin: perennial; native

Zone/Habitat: riparian deciduous, montane, subalpine at 6,000-9,000' (1,830-2,745 m); open ponderosa pine forests, under firs or maples, canyons, partial shade

Range: most of the eastern two-thirds of Arizona

Notes: This honeysuckle is one of many species of wildflowers in Arizona that have reddish tubular flowers pollinated by any of the 13 species of hummingbirds found in the state. Researchers have discovered that hummingbirds in the White Mountains carry pollen simultaneously from as many as four different wildflower species with similar-looking, tubular red blooms. Differences in the tube shapes and lengths of the flower parts determine where on the bodies of the birds the pollen is deposited. Thus, the pollen right for a flower species is brushed off on the next corresponding species.

FLOWER TYPE	LEAF TYPE	LEAF ATTACHMENT	FRUIT
Tube	Simple	Opposite	Berry

THURBER DESERT-HONEYSUCKLE
Anisacanthus thurberi

Family: Acanthus (Acanthaceae)

Height: 3-6' (.9-1.8 m); shrub

Flower: slim tubular reddish orange or orange flowers, 1-2" (2.5-5 cm) long, have fused petals flaring into 4 long pointed lobes that curl backward, protruding orange and white flower parts and green sepals

Leaf: stalkless elliptical leaves, 1-2½" (2.5-6 cm) long, with smooth edges and pointed tips; usually in dense clusters

Bloom: Mar-Jun and Oct-Dec

Cycle/Origin: perennial; native

Zone/Habitat: desert scrub, interior chaparral, oak/pinyon pine/juniper woods, riparian deciduous at 1,500-5,500' (460-1,675 m); canyons, along washes

Range: throughout Arizona, except the north central part of the state

Notes: This common flowering shrub is found only in Arizona and New Mexico in the United States, but ranges south into northern Mexico. Also called Chuparosa, meaning "hummingbird" in Spanish, a name commonly used for all plants that attract hummingbirds. There are more species of hummingbirds found in Arizona than in any other state, making planting flowers for these tiny "jewels" popular. A good choice for wildlife gardens, it requires well-drained soil, a little water, full sun and is hardy to 15°F (-9°C).

FLOWER TYPE	LEAF TYPE	LEAF ATTACHMENT	LEAF ATTACHMENT
Tube	Simple	Opposite	Whorl

HUMMINGBIRD'S TRUMPET
Epilobium canum

Family: Evening-primrose (Onagraceae)

Height: 12-24" (30-61 cm); shrub

Flower: bright orange tubular flowers, 1½" (4 cm) long, flaring at mouth into 4 wrinkled petals and protruding reddish orange flower parts; each petal is notched in the center; flowers grouped toward top of stems

Leaf: elliptical, dark green leaves, ½-2" (1-5 cm) long, are hairy, sticky, with edges finely toothed; lower leaves opposite, upper leaves alternate and much smaller

Fruit: cylindrical beaked hairy capsule, 1" (2.5 cm) long

Bloom: Jun-Dec

Cycle/Origin: perennial; native

Zone/Habitat: interior chaparral, oak/pinyon pine/juniper woods, riparian deciduous at 2,500-7,000' (760-2,135 m); moist seeps, rocky slopes, canyons, arroyos

Range: throughout Arizona, except the northeastern and southwestern corners of the state

Notes: A hummingbird magnet, this flower is often grown in desert wildlife gardens in moist soil near birdbaths or along a water feature. Can tolerate drier conditions in cooler climates. In the wild, it is easily found in the fall along washes in Molino Basin Campground and Bear Canyon Picnic Area in the Santa Catalina Mountains, north of Tucson. Hummingbirds defend these rich nectar sources from each other, competing for territories that include the most blooms.

FLOWER TYPE	LEAF TYPE	LEAF ATTACHMENT	LEAF ATTACHMENT	FRUIT
Tube	Simple	Alternate	Opposite	Pod

FISHHOOK BARREL
Ferocactus wislizeni

Family: Cactus (Cactaceae)

Height: 1-4' (30-122 cm)

Flower: cup-shaped orange flowers, 1½-3½" (4-9 cm) wide, form a ring at the top of cactus; many sharp-tipped, wavy-edged, overlapping petals, each with a darker midline stripe, surround a wide yellow center

Spines: 20-25 spines, 1½-2" (4-5 cm) long, in clusters; each cluster has 4 stout central pinkish spines flattened and ribbed, with longest slightly hooked at end; 12-20 thread-like whitish gray radial spines; shallow notch in the rib just above each cluster

Fruit: cylindrical yellow pod, 2" (5 cm) long, with wrinkled thick fleshy walls, spineless, brown tuft at top

Bloom: Jul-Sep

Cycle/Origin: perennial; native

Zone/Habitat: desert scrub, grassland and low oak woodlands at 1,000-5,300' (305-1,615 m); flats, arroyos, slopes

Range: southern half of Arizona

Notes: A wide barrel-shaped cactus with a single fleshy green stem that has 20-30 ribs. The ribs run lengthwise, with deep grooves between. After rain, the ribs become wider and the grooves shallower as the cactus fills with water. Its hooked central spines were used as fishing hooks by American Indians. Older plants can grow to 10 feet (3 m) tall. Like all barrel cacti, it tends to lean southwest.

FLOWER TYPE

Regular

LEAF TYPE

Spines

FRUIT

Pod

INDIAN BLANKET
Gaillardia pulchella

Family: Aster (Asteraceae)

Height: 2-24" (5-61 cm)

Flower: daisy-like, tricolored flower head, 2-3" (5-7.5 cm) wide, made up of 8-14 triangular (orange, red or purple) petals with 3-lobed (usually yellow or orange) tips surrounding a domed maroon center

Leaf: narrowly oblong or spoon-shaped leaves, ½-3½" (1-9 cm) long, are fuzzy above with usually smooth edges; upper leaves smaller and clasping; alternately attached to multi-branched, sticky-haired stem

Bloom: Apr-Sep

Cycle/Origin: usually annual, sometimes perennial or biennial; native

Zone/Habitat: grasslands, pinyon pine/juniper woodlands, montane at 3,500-6,000' (1,065-1,830 m); disturbed ground, along roads and railroads, forest clearings

Range: eastern half of Arizona

Notes: Also called Firewheel because the flower resembles a child's pinwheel, with its maroon center surrounded by an orange or red ring that, in turn, is encircled by a ring of yellow. Readily self-seeds and forms large colorful masses of flowers that blanket the ground. Many state highway departments plant this eye-catching flower along roads. Often grown in wildflower gardens since it needs little care and the flowers last a long time.

FLOWER TYPE	LEAF TYPE	LEAF ATTACHMENT
	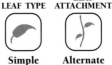	
Composite	**Simple**	**Alternate**

DESERT MARIPOSA LILY
Calochortus kennedyi

Family: Lily (Liliaceae)

Height: 4-16" (10-40 cm)

Flower: bright orange flower, 3" (7.5 cm) wide; tulip-shaped with 3 broad petals, each with fringed blotch at base; 3 narrow sepals; purple and orange center

Leaf: basal leaves, 4-8" (10-20 cm) long, are grass-like, folded lengthwise and wither before the plant blooms; few stem leaves

Fruit: lance-shaped capsule, 1½-2½" (4-6 cm) long, is purplish green with white stripes and turns brown

Bloom: Mar-May, after good winter rains

Cycle/Origin: perennial; native

Zone/Habitat: desert scrub and grasslands at 2,000-5,000' (610-1,525 m); open or brushy areas, hillsides, flats

Range: western third and southernmost quarter of Arizona

Notes: "Mariposa" means "butterfly" in Spanish and refers to the wing-like movement of the colorful petals in a breeze. Grows on dry rocky hillsides. Often mistaken by springtime hikers for the four-petaled California Poppy (pg. 341) from a distance, but the flowers of Desert Mariposa Lily are larger and have three petals. The less common, yellow-flowered variation of Desert Mariposa Lily may be mistaken for Golden Mariposa Lily (*C. aureus*) (not shown), which has a thin dark crescent on the bases of the petals.

FLOWER TYPE	LEAF TYPE	LEAF ATTACHMENT	LEAF ATTACHMENT	FRUIT
Regular	Simple	Alternate	Basal	Pod

fruit

BUTTERFLYWEED
Asclepias tuberosa

Family: Milkweed (Asclepiadaceae)

Height: 12-24" (30-61 cm)

Flower: large flat cluster, 2-3" (5-7.5 cm) wide, of small, deep orange flowers; each flower, ⅜" (.9 cm) wide, with downward-curving petals; flower color varies from all yellow to red

Leaf: hairy lance-shaped leaves, 2-6" (5-15 cm) long, widen near tips and are toothless; hairy stem

Fruit: erect narrow green pod, turning brown, 6" (15 cm) long, is covered with fine hairs; pods are in small clusters and have large brown seeds with silken "parachutes" to carry away each seed

Bloom: May-Sep

Cycle/Origin: perennial; native

Zone/Habitat: grasslands and montane at 4,000-8,000' (1,220-1,830 m); clearings in pine forests

Range: northern half and southeastern part of Arizona

Notes: Also called Butterfly Milkweed. Found in clumps, this true milkweed lacks milky sap; instead, its stem and leaves contain clear sap. Species name *tuberosa* refers to its large taproot, which makes it nearly impossible to transplant. Can be grown from seed. Single stems branch only near the top and flower clusters harbor up to 25 flowers. Roots and stems have been used in folk medicine. A host plant for Gray Hairstreak and Monarch butterfly caterpillars.

CLUSTER TYPE	FLOWER TYPE	LEAF TYPE	LEAF ATTACHMENT	FRUIT
Flat	Irregular	Simple	Alternate	Pod

pink form

CALICHE GLOBE MALLOW
Sphaeralcea laxa

Family: Mallow (Malvaceae)

Height: 12-36" (30-91 cm)

Flower: loose spike cluster, 6-12" (15-30 cm) long, of slightly cupped, bright reddish orange flowers, 1-1½" (2.5-4 cm) wide; 5 slightly wrinkled, fan-shaped petals surround a star-shaped green center with dark maroon male flower parts (anthers)

Leaf: 3-lobed, triangular or heart-shaped, grayish green leaves, ½-2" (1-5 cm) long, have scalloped edges; tiny star-shaped white hairs on leaves and stems

Fruit: pod-like tan container, ¼" (.6 cm) wide, shaped like half an orange, has 12-14 pie-shaped segments

Bloom: Mar-Nov, mostly in spring, but also after heavy rain

Cycle/Origin: perennial; native

Zone/Habitat: desert scrub and grasslands at 2,000-6,000' (610-1,830 m); flats, mesas

Range: eastern two-thirds of Arizona

Notes: The most common globe mallow found in the deserts near Tucson, but Desert Globe Mallow (pg. 71) is most often cultivated in highway medians and landscaping in that area. Unlike Desert Globe Mallow's orange anthers, Caliche Globe Mallow anthers are always maroon or pink, while petal color varies from orange to pink, lavender or white (see inset). Grows in alkaline soils containing a hard layer of calcium carbonate (caliche) beneath the surface.

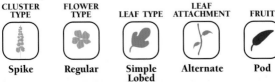

CLUSTER TYPE	FLOWER TYPE	LEAF TYPE	LEAF ATTACHMENT	FRUIT
Spike	Regular	Simple Lobed	Alternate	Pod

DESERT GLOBE MALLOW
Sphaeralcea ambigua

Family: Mallow (Malvaceae)

Height: 20-36" (50-91 cm)

Flower: wand-like spike cluster, 6-12" (15-30 cm) long, of many bowl-shaped, light orange flowers, ⅝-2" (1.5-5 cm) wide; 5 triangular orange petals with pale yellow bases and wavy outer edges surround a green center with yellow male flower parts (anthers)

Leaf: triangular, grayish green leaves, ⅝-2" (1.5-5 cm) long, are deeply veined, 3-lobed and have scalloped margins; upper leaves much smaller; star-shaped white hairs cover leaves and stems

Fruit: pod-like tan container, ¼" (.6 cm) wide, shaped like half an orange, is segmented and has tiny seeds

Bloom: mostly Mar-Apr, any time of year after heavy rain

Cycle/Origin: perennial; native

Zone/Habitat: desert scrub below 3,500' (1,065 m); sandy washes

Range: western two-thirds of Arizona

Notes: The most common globe mallow found east of Phoenix and along the Pinal Pioneer Parkway (Highway 79) from Tucson to Florence, Arizona. Flowers can be white, pale pink, lavender or red; the male flower parts (anthers) are always yellow. Grows in many-stemmed clumps with showy flower stalks above the mound of foliage. Bighorn sheep and domestic sheep and goats eat the leaves.

CLUSTER TYPE	FLOWER TYPE	LEAF TYPE	LEAF ATTACHMENT	FRUIT
Spike	Regular	Simple Lobed	Alternate	Pod

SMALL-FLOWERED GLOBE MALLOW
Sphaeralcea parvifolia

Family: Mallow (Malvaceae)

Height: 24-36" (61-91 cm)

Flower: straight spike cluster, 12-18" (30-45 cm) long, of whorls of many cup-shaped, bright orange flowers, 1" (2.5 cm) wide; 5 heart-shaped orange petals with pale yellow bases surround a green center with yellow male flower parts (anthers)

Leaf: small, broadly triangular, grayish green leaves, ½-1½" (1-4 cm) long, have extremely wavy margins; upper surfaces have white glands and deep veins

Fruit: flattened, disk-shaped pod is green, turning tan, ¼" (.6 cm) wide, and is segmented

Bloom: May-Sep

Cycle/Origin: perennial; native

Zone/Habitat: desert scrub, oak/pinyon pine/juniper woodlands, 3,500-7,000' (1,065-2,135 m); low canyons

Range: northern half of Arizona

Notes: Especially common in canyon country such as the Four Corners area of northeastern Arizona. Often forms dense colonies. Although heat and drought tolerant, in years following heavy winter rains it blooms for weeks, carpeting large areas along roads with orange. The Latin *parvifolia* means "little leaf" and fits this plant to a "T," as the curly leaves are the smallest among globe mallows in the state.

CLUSTER TYPE	FLOWER TYPE	LEAF TYPE	LEAF ATTACHMENT	FRUIT
Spike	Regular	Simple Lobed	Alternate	Pod

73

SPREADING DOGBANE
Apocynum androsaemifolium

Family: Dogbane (Apocynaceae)

Height: 12-20" (30-50 cm)

Flower: groups of 2-10 pink-to-white flowers on stalks above leaves; each bell-shaped flower, ⅓" (.8 cm) long, can be white with pink stripes within the bell

Leaf: oval leaves, 2-4" (5-10 cm) long, pale whitish green and slightly hairy below, toothless wavy margins

Fruit: thin pod, 3-8" (7.5-20 cm) long, opens along 1 side, revealing seeds attached to long tufts of white fuzz

Bloom: Jun-Aug

Cycle/Origin: perennial; native

Zone/Habitat: interior chaparral, riparian deciduous, montane at 7,000-9,000' (2,135-2,745 m); clearings, slopes

Range: northern half and southeastern part of Arizona

Notes: A perennial with a single main stem branching into many "spreading" stems. A close relative of the milkweed, it produces a thick white milky juice in its stems and leaves. This juice contains cardiac glycosides, which cause hot flashes, rapid heartbeat and fatigue. Five thin sensitive scales in the flower's throat ooze sweet nectar, which attracts flies. The scale will turn inward when a fly brushes against it, trapping the insect. When dried and peeled, the fibrous bark makes a strong cord, which was once used by American Indians for fishing and trapping. The same fibers are selectively used by orioles as nest-building material.

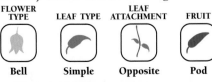

FLOWER TYPE	LEAF TYPE	LEAF ATTACHMENT	FRUIT
Bell	Simple	Opposite	Pod

TENLEAF WOOD SORREL
Oxalis decaphylla

Family: Wood Sorrel (Oxalidaceae)

Height: 3-5" (7.5-13 cm)

Flower: pink flowers, ½" (1 cm) wide, with yellow throats; each bloom has 5 broad streaked petals that are pink on outer half and fused at the white base, curving out around a white and yellow center

Leaf: basal leaves, 2" (5 cm) wide, appearing like a closed umbrella, are divided into 4-10 folded heart-shaped leaflets hung upside down by tips from a central point on a long stalk; leaflets are green and edged with maroon above, and are maroon below

Bloom: Jun-Aug

Cycle/Origin: perennial; native

Zone/Habitat: oak/pinyon pine/juniper woodlands, montane and subalpine at 5,000-9,500' (1,525-2,895 m); among grasses, moist deep loamy soils

Range: northern half of Arizona, except the northwestern corner; the southeastern quarter of the state

Notes: The bulbs of this plant make up a large portion of the diet of Montezuma Quail, which are dependent upon Tenleaf Wood Sorrel being plentiful in its habitat. This colorful quail is found in Arizona and New Mexico, the only two states in the U.S. where this plant is known to occur. Foliage of plants in the genus *Oxalis* contains oxalic acid, which is secreted as sharp calcium oxalate crystals.

FLOWER TYPE	LEAF TYPE	LEAF ATTACHMENT
Regular	Compound	Basal

PINEYWOODS GERANIUM
Geranium caespitosum

Family: Geranium (Geraniaceae)

Height: 4-36" (10-91 cm)

Flower: pink-to-lilac flower, ½" (1 cm) wide, has 5 backward-drooping petals with dark pink veins, 5 sepals with thread-like tips, greenish flower parts

Leaf: hand-shaped hairy basal leaves, 1½" (4 cm) wide, pinkish edges, 5 toothed lobes; red stems

Fruit: stiff green container, ½" (1 cm) long, shaped like a crane's bill, contains 1 seed tipped with an elongated tail that coils at maturity

Bloom: May-Oct

Cycle/Origin: perennial; native

Zone/Habitat: montane at 6,000-9,000' (1,830-2,745 m); among Ponderosa Pines, meadows, along trails, dry soils

Range: northern half and southeastern corner of Arizona

Notes: Species name *caespitosum* is Latin for "growing in clumps" and describes how this small plant is found. Genus name *Geranium* is from the Greek *geranos*, meaning "crane" and refers to the shape of the fruit, which resembles a crane's bill. The seed has a tail that coils at maturity and straightens out with rainfall, which forces the pointed seed into the soil. The leaves are fragrant when crushed. American Indians traditionally made a concoction from the root to treat diarrhea. Different from Richardson Geranium (pg. 223), which prefers moist soils, has white petals and is purple veined.

FLOWER TYPE	LEAF TYPE	LEAF ATTACHMENT	LEAF ATTACHMENT	FRUIT
Regular	Simple Lobed	Opposite	Basal	Pod

LITTLELEAF RATANY
Krameria erecta

Family: Ratany (Krameriaceae)

Height: 12-36" (30-91 cm); shrub

Flower: dark pink or purple flowers, ¾" (2 cm) wide, have 5 lance-shaped, fuzzy, pink petal-like sepals bent downward (lower sepal is cupped forward) around the tiny erect magenta petals with yellowish green bases and protruding magenta or green flower parts

Leaf: fuzzy, whitish green leaves, ⅛-½" (.3-1 cm) long, are short and narrow with pointed tips and reddish prickles; oppositely attached along woody stems

Fruit: fuzzy, egg-shaped, greenish cream pod, ½" (1 cm) long, has bright red spines with minute barbs

Bloom: Apr-Nov

Cycle/Origin: perennial; native

Zone/Habitat: desert scrub, grasslands below 5,000' (1,525 m); rocky slopes and ridges, among grasses

Range: throughout Arizona, except the northeastern corner

Notes: A small, multi-branched, sprawling gray shrub with inconspicuous leaves and oddly shaped flowers. All species in *Krameria* are semiparasitic, obtaining part of their nutrients through the roots of nearby plants. Instead of producing nectar, attracts insect pollinators by making oil, which is collected by bees and mixed with pollen to make food for their larvae. The Tohono O'odham Indians extracted a red juice from the roots to make a dye.

FLOWER TYPE	LEAF TYPE	LEAF ATTACHMENT	FRUIT
Irregular	Simple	Opposite	Pod

81

TRAILING FOUR O'CLOCK
Allionia incarnata

Family: Four O'clock (Nyctaginaceae)

Height: 1-5' (30-152 cm); vine

Flower: appears to be a regular flower, 1" (2.5 cm) wide, composed of 9 flat, 2-lobed, purplish pink petals surrounding a magenta-and-yellow center, but is actually made up of 3 irregular flowers on a short stalk growing from a leaf attachment

Leaf: oval leaves, ¾-3" (2-7.5 cm) long, dull green above and gray below, blunt bases, usually pointed tips, edges smooth or wavy; pairs of leaves of unequal size; sticky, hairy stem

Bloom: Mar-Oct, in almost any season after rainfall

Cycle/Origin: annual, perennial; native

Zone/Habitat: desert scrub, grasslands below 6,000' (1,830 m); along roads and washes, slopes, mesas

Range: throughout

Notes: This ground-hugging vine has what appears to be one regular round flat flower, but is actually three irregular flowers that bloom at the same time. It blooms after rain in all but the coldest weather. Occurs wherever there is sandy soil, often in disturbed areas. The sticky, hairy leaves are usually dotted with sand. American Indians used this plant as a poultice to treat swelling and fever, and brewed it into a tea to treat diarrhea or kidney disease. Trailing Four-O'clock occurs throughout the Southwest.

FLOWER TYPE

Irregular

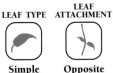

LEAF TYPE

Simple

LEAF ATTACHMENT

Opposite

DESERT FIVE SPOT
Eremalche rotundifolia

Family: Mallow (Malvaceae)

Height: 3-24" (7.5-61 cm)

Flower: spherical pink-to-purple flowers, 1" (2.5 cm) wide, of 5 round petals surrounding many yellow male flowers parts (stamens); each petal is cream inside with a reddish blotch at the base

Leaf: round to heart-shaped, green or red leaves, ½-2½" (1-6 cm) wide, have short bristly hairs and irregularly scalloped edges, on long reddish leafstalks

Fruit: round disk-shaped tan pods, 1" (2.5 cm) wide, with 25-35 pie-shaped sections

Bloom: Mar-May

Cycle/Origin: annual; native

Zone/Habitat: desert scrub below 4,000' (1,220 m); flats, lower mountain slopes (bajadas), mesas

Range: westernmost quarter of Arizona

Notes: A common spring ephemeral of the Mojave Desert named for the five red spots found inside each bloom (see inset). Also called Chinese Lantern, as the flowers are globe-shaped with a small opening at the top and appear to glow when light shines through the delicate petals. The blossoms group together in the leaf junctions, opening in the afternoon and closing at night. The leaves of this short-lived, low-growing annual track the sun, turning to get the maximum amount of sunlight to make food (photosynthesis).

FLOWER TYPE	LEAF TYPE	LEAF ATTACHMENT	FRUIT
	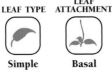		
Regular	Simple	Basal	Pod

Rock Hibiscus
Hibiscus denudatus

Family: Mallow (Malvaceae)

Height: 12-24" (30-61 cm)

Flower: slightly cupped, pale pink (can be white)-to-deep lavender flowers, 1-1½" (2.5-4 cm) wide, have 5 slightly overlapping, broad wavy petals with pink-streaked bases around a pink center

Leaf: rounded triangular to oblong, grayish green leaves, ½-1" (1-2.5 cm) long, are densely hairy with toothed edges; sparse and alternate along the several straggly stems

Fruit: 5-parted, star-shaped tan capsule with hairy seeds

Bloom: Jan-Oct, but nearly year-round after rain

Cycle/Origin: perennial; native

Zone/Habitat: desert scrub below 4,500' (1,370 m); rocky slopes, canyons, among creosotebushes, in sandy washes

Range: southern third of Arizona

Notes: Mallows are easily identified by the central column of fused male flower parts (stamens), which is usually some shade of red in Rock Hibiscus. The leaves are always sparse and sometimes missing altogether when the plant is flowering. It blooms following rain throughout most of the year. In its westernmost range, where it is called Paleface, the flowers are white with red centers. Farther eastward, the blossoms are pink; they are purple in its easternmost range. The pink form grows in Saguaro National Park, near Tucson.

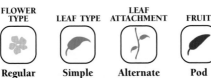

FLOWER TYPE	LEAF TYPE	LEAF ATTACHMENT	FRUIT
Regular	Simple	Alternate	Pod

fruit

ARIZONA FISHHOOK PINCUSHION
Mammillaria grahamii

Family: Cactus (Cactaceae)

Height: 2-6" (5-15 cm)

Flower: pink or pink and white, star-shaped flowers, 1-1½" (2.5-4 cm) wide, form ring at the top of cactus; many overlapping pointed petals, each with a dark pink midline, surround an orange and green center

Spines: 26-35 spines, ¼-1" (.6-2.5 cm) long, in clusters; each cluster has 3-4 longer, central, reddish brown-to-black spines (1 or more hooked at tips) and many short, bristle-like, whitish or tan radial spines

Fruit: fleshy green pod, turning red, ½-1" (1-2.5 cm) long

Bloom: Jun-Jul, buds in early spring, but delays flowering until after first summer rains

Cycle/Origin: perennial; native

Zone/Habitat: desert scrub, grasslands, interior chaparral and oak/pinyon pine/juniper woodlands at 1,000-5,000' (305-1,525 m); under cholla cacti, rocky soils

Range: southern half of Arizona

Notes: Of the many pincushion cacti in Arizona, this is the most common and widespread. It has fine pin-like projecting spines and spherical or cylindrical short stems that occur alone or in clumps. "Fishhook" in the common name is for the hooked central spines. The bright pink flowers appear large for its size. The green stems are obscured by the radial spines, so it appears overall gray.

FLOWER TYPE	LEAF TYPE	FRUIT
Regular	Spines	Pod

fruit

ARIZONA ROSE
Rosa woodsii

Family: Rose (Rosaceae)

Height: 4-10' (1.2-3 m); shrub

Flower: groups of 2-5 light pink flowers, 1½" (4 cm) wide, of 5 bluntly oval petals surrounding a bright yellow center; backed by 5 narrowly pointed green sepals

Leaf: dark green leaves, 2-5" (5-13 cm) long, divided into 5-11 oval leaflets, 1-2" (2.5-5 cm) long; toothed leaflets tipped with sticky glands; thorny stems

Fruit: hard, oval, berry-like green fruit, turning red when ripe, ½" (1 cm) wide

Bloom: May-Jul

Cycle/Origin: perennial; native

Zone/Habitat: riparian deciduous and montane at 4,000-9,000' (1,220-2,745 m); along streams, open areas in ponderosa pine forests, roadside ditches, moist soils

Range: northern half and southeastern quarter of Arizona

Notes: Arizona Rose is the most widespread and abundant wild rose in the state. Its stout thorns, thick at the base and curving to a hooked point, resemble a cat's claws. The red fruits (called rose hips) contain large amounts of vitamin C and protein and can be made into jams, jellies and wine. If you live in the mountains of Arizona, plant this rose to attract wildlife. The rose hips persist over winter and are a food source for wildlife, elk and deer eat the leaves, and the older woody stems provide cover for birds and small animals.

FLOWER TYPE	LEAF TYPE	LEAF ATTACHMENT	FRUIT
Regular	Compound	Alternate	Berry

YELLOW-SPINE THISTLE
Cirsium ochrocentrum

Family: Aster (Asteraceae)

Height: 12-36" (30-91 cm)

Flower: broad and rayless flower head, ¾-3" (2-7.5 cm) wide, is pink or red; bloom made of thin tubular disk flowers sitting on a spherical green base of very spiny bracts; spines point upward

Leaf: grayish green basal leaves, 4-12" (10-30 cm) long, narrowly elliptical, covered with matted white hairs; each lobe or tooth ends in a long yellow spine; the bases of stem leaves form wings

Bloom: May-Oct

Cycle/Origin: perennial, biennial; native

Zone/Habitat: pinyon pine/juniper woods at 4,500-8,000' (1,370-2,440 m); roadsides, rangelands, disturbed areas, woodland clearings

Range: northern half and southern edge of Arizona

Notes: The long erect leaves grow close to the stem, allowing the densely hairy white undersides to be seen and making Yellow-spine Thistle easy to identify from a distance. One of the longest-spined thistles in Arizona; it also has the most spines. The flowers attract many types of insects. Traditionally, the peeled stems and the young leaves were cooked as greens, tea was made by steeping the older leaves, and the roots were eaten raw or cooked. Spreads rapidly by its deep creeping roots. Considered a noxious weed in California.

FLOWER TYPE	LEAF TYPE	LEAF ATTACHMENT	LEAF ATTACHMENT
Composite	Simple Lobed	Alternate	Basal

BIRD'S FOOT MORNING GLORY
Ipomoea ternifolia

Family: Morning Glory (Convolvulaceae)

Height: 12-36" (30-91 cm); vine

Flower: trumpet-shaped, purplish pink flowers, 2" (5 cm) wide, made up of fused petals with darker pink bases, flaring widely around a white center; 1-2 blooms per stalk attached at a leaf junction (axis)

Leaf: hand-shaped leaves divided into 3-5 narrow lobes, 1-3" (2.5-7.5 cm) long, on stalks, alternate along the twining stem

Bloom: Jun-Oct

Cycle/Origin: annual; native

Zone/Habitat: desert scrub and grasslands at 2,500-4,500' (760-1,370 m); along washes, among grasses, in shrubs, flats, mesas

Range: southeastern quarter of Arizona

Notes: These showy, delicate-looking flowers don't appear until after the monsoon rains. The vines trail along the ground or twine in shrubs a few feet high. Blooms are sometimes pure white or purple, always opening in early morning and wilting by afternoon. The leaves are divided into narrow lobes resembling the three toes of a bird's foot, thus the common name. This species often hybridizes with the similar Crestrib Morning Glory (*I. costellata*) (not shown).

FLOWER TYPE	LEAF TYPE	LEAF ATTACHMENT
Tube	Simple Lobed	Alternate

NEW MEXICO THISTLE
Cirsium neomexicanum

Family: Aster (Asteraceae)

Height: 2-10' (.6-3 m)

Flower: pink-to-pale lavender flower head, 2-3" (5-7.5 cm) wide, disk-shaped, of thin tubular disk flowers on a spherical green base of spiny bracts that narrows near its top; outer bracts pointing downward

Leaf: oblong leaves, 2½-14" (6-36 cm) long, dark green, each lobe ending in a sharp spine, stalkless or with winged leafstalks; upper stem leaves are much smaller, clasping; stem branches above the middle

Bloom: Mar-Jul

Cycle/Origin: perennial, biennial; native

Zone/Habitat: desert scrub, grasslands and pinyon pine/juniper woodlands at 1,000-6,500' (305-1,980 m); slopes, plains, mesas, roadsides, canyons

Range: throughout

Notes: A colorful weed often noticed along highways in Arizona, this is possibly the most common and widespread of the 17 species of thistle in the state. The usually pink or purple flowers can be white on some plants. Thistles are generally disliked for their spines and tendency to invade pastures (cattle avoid the plant). However, thistles are a good resource for wildlife. Hummingbirds and butterflies love the nectar. The seeds are a favorite food of the Lesser Goldfinch, which raises its young in late summer. This bird lines its nest with the thistledown produced after the thistles flower.

FLOWER TYPE	LEAF TYPE	LEAF ATTACHMENT	LEAF ATTACHMENT
Composite	Simple Lobed	Alternate	Clasping

PINK-FLOWERED HEDGEHOG
Echinocereus fasciculatus

Family: Cactus (Cactaceae)

Height: 7-16" (18-40 cm)

Flower: 1 or several large, showy, bright pink-to-purplish pink flowers, 3-4" (7.5-10 cm) wide, are wide and cup-shaped, have overlapping pointed wavy petals surrounding a yellow and green center; outer petals brownish with a dark midline; found atop stems

Spines: clusters of 8-16 dark-tipped, gray-to-white spines, ⅕-3" (.5-7.5 cm) long; each cluster has 1-3 straight, outward- or downward-pointing central spines (1 is largest) and 7-15 shorter spreading radial spines

Fruit: fleshy spiny red pod, 1" (2.5 cm) long, pink pulp

Bloom: Mar-Apr

Cycle/Origin: perennial; native

Zone/Habitat: desert scrub, grasslands, interior chaparral at 2,000-5,000' (610-1,525 m); under shrubs or in the open

Range: southeastern corner of Arizona

Notes: In Arizona, *Echinocereus* has six species of small, ribbed, cylindrical hedgehog cacti. This common species is found only in southeastern Arizona, southwestern New Mexico and northern Mexico. It grows in clumps of 5-24 unbranching stout stems. The dark-tipped gray spines are uneven in length, and each cluster has one longest central spine that is straight, setting this hedgehog apart from other species. The fruit is edible and relished by wildlife.

FLOWER TYPE

Regular

LEAF TYPE

Spines

FRUIT

Pod

fruit

FILAREE
Erodium cicutarium

Family: Geranium (Geraniaceae)

Height: 4-20" (10-50 cm)

Flower: loose flat cluster, 1" (2.5 cm) wide, of 2-12 pink-to-violet flowers; each small flower is ¼" (.6 cm) wide and has 5 oval petals backed by 5 pointed hairy sepals; each sepal is green with white lines

Leaf: lance- or kidney-shaped, reddish or dark green basal leaves, 2-10" (5-25 cm) long, in a prostrate rosette, fern-like, fuzzy, divided into lobed leaflets

Fruit: erect green capsule, turning brown, ¾-2" (2-5 cm) long, long and pointed, shaped like the beak of a heron or stork, twisting into a spiral when dry

Bloom: Feb-Jul

Cycle/Origin: annual, biennial; non-native, from southern Europe

Zone/Habitat: all life zones below 7,000' (2,135 m); roadsides

Range: throughout

Notes: Filaree is often the first weed to overtake any disturbed soil, such as overgrazed rangelands, and can reduce crop production. Also named Redstem Stork's Bill for the shape of the seedpod. The pod curls into a corkscrew shape when dry, looking like a tail on the seed; it untwists when moistened by rain, which drives the single seed into the ground. Seeds are eaten by harvester ants and birds. Desert tortoises, bighorn sheep, deer and livestock eat the foliage.

CLUSTER TYPE	FLOWER TYPE	LEAF TYPE	LEAF ATTACHMENT	LEAF ATTACHMENT	FRUIT

Flat	Regular	Compound	Opposite	Basal	Pod

WILD MINT
Mentha arvensis

Family: Mint (Lamiaceae)

Height: 6-24" (15-61 cm)

Flower: open round cluster, 1" (2.5 cm) wide, of small pale lilac-pink or white flowers; each flower, ¼" (.6 cm) long; flower cluster encircles the square stem where each pair of leaves attach

Leaf: pairs of lance-shaped leaves, 1-2" (2.5-5 cm) long, tapering at both ends, toothed margins; leaves get smaller near the top of plant; leaves have a strong odor when crushed

Bloom: Jul-Oct

Cycle/Origin: perennial; native

Zone/Habitat: oak/pinyon pine/juniper woods, riparian deciduous and montane at 5,000-9,000' (1,525-2,745 m); moist forests, along streams and lakes

Range: northeastern two-thirds of Arizona and scattered locations in southern half of the state

Notes: Native to Arizona, and the only native mint in *Mentha* (genus of the so-called "true mints") in the United States. Sometimes called American Wild Mint. Because plants have no way to eliminate waste, byproduct chemicals are stored in the leaves in the form of essential oils. These oils, which give the leaves of this plant a minty smell and taste, have been used as flavoring in beverages and other foods.

CLUSTER TYPE	FLOWER TYPE	LEAF TYPE	LEAF ATTACHMENT
			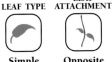
Round	Irregular	Simple	Opposite

fruit

FAIRY DUSTER
Calliandra eriophylla

Family: Pea or Bean (Fabaceae)

Height: 12-36" (30-91 cm); shrub

Flower: round, fuzzy, pink-and-white cluster, 1-2" (2.5-5 cm) wide; each cluster consists mainly of long male flower parts (stamens) with yellow tips

Leaf: dark green leaves, 1-1½" (2.5-4 cm) long, divided into 2-4 pairs of leaflets and again into 7-9 tiny oval subleaflets; bulbous gray stem; usually evergreen, but can drop leaves during cold or drought

Fruit: flat pea-like green pod, turning reddish brown, 2-4" (5-10 cm) long, is fuzzy with thickened edges; splits lengthwise with a loud popping sound, forcefully dispersing the seeds

Bloom: Oct-May

Cycle/Origin: perennial; native

Zone/Habitat: desert scrub, grasslands below 5,000' (1,525 m); flats, rocky slopes, along washes

Range: throughout, except the northeastern quarter

Notes: Thornless or with a few paired thorns on its stems, Fairy Duster is a low-growing branching shrub. When in bloom, it is covered with fluffy pink balls with yellow dots that appear to float above the surface of the flower. The flowers attract butterflies and hummingbirds; deer and javelinas (pig-like animals) eat the leaves. The curly open seedpods remain on the shrub for months.

CLUSTER TYPE	FLOWER TYPE	LEAF TYPE	LEAF ATTACHMENT	FRUIT
Round	Irregular	Twice Compound	Alternate	Pod

ARIZONA VALERIAN
Valeriana arizonica

Family: Valerian (Valerianaceae)

Height: 8-14" (20-36 cm)

Flower: star-shaped, pale pink-to-lavender flowers, 1" (2.5 cm) long; each tubular flower has 5 petals around the darker pink throat and protruding pink or white male flower parts (stamens); blossoms in a spiky round cluster, 2" (5 cm) wide

Leaf: spoon-shaped basal leaves, 2½-6½" (6-15 cm) long, are smooth and on long stalks; a few shorter arrow-shaped stem leaves have 2-3 pairs of lobes and clasp the hollow stems

Bloom: Apr-Jul

Cycle/Origin: perennial; native

Zone/Habitat: montane and subalpine at 4,500-8,000' (1,370-2,440 m); coniferous forests, moist rich soils

Range: northern half and southeastern quarter of Arizona

Notes: The pretty, frilly pink flowers of this mountain wildflower top the almost leafless branching stems above the basal rosette of dark green leaves. Often found along mountain streams, this plant can be easily seen along Oak Creek, near Sedona, Arizona. It is an attractive plant for moist places in the garden. The genus name *Valeriana* may be from the Latin word *valere*, which means "to be healthy and strong," referring to the use of these plants in folk medicine to treat nervousness and hysteria.

CLUSTER TYPE	FLOWER TYPE	LEAF TYPE	LEAF TYPE	LEAF ATTACHMENT	LEAF ATTACHMENT
Round	Tube	Simple	Simple Lobed	Opposite	Basal

EASTERN MOJAVE BUCKWHEAT
Eriogonum fasciculatum

Family: Buckwheat (Polygonaceae)

Height: 1-5' (30-152 cm); shrub

Flower: numerous fuzzy pink-to-white flowers in a densely packed flat cluster, ½-8" (1-20 cm) wide; each tiny flower is only ⅛" (.3 cm) wide

Leaf: leathery narrow oblong leaves, ¼-½" (.6-1 cm) long, with margins rolled inward; 1 to many leaves at each node of stem; reddish brown stems erect or sprawling, turning grayish and woody with age

Bloom: Feb-Jun

Cycle/Origin: perennial; native

Zone/Habitat: desert scrub and grasslands at 1,000-4,500' (305-1,370 m); along roads and washes, slopes

Range: western two-thirds of Arizona

Notes: Many butterflies feed on the nectar of Eastern Mojave Buckwheat, and several species of butterfly caterpillars are dependent upon the foliage. Wild bees and honeybees also visit the flower, and it is an important wild nectar source used for honey production. Often cultivated in rock or butterfly gardens, this small, open, multi-stemmed shrub is easily grown from seed. American Indians traditionally used the plant medicinally to treat a variety of illnesses, including heart problems. Scientific studies have proven other species in the *Eriogonum* genus contain compounds that are beneficial to the heart. Also known as California Buckwheat.

CLUSTER TYPE	FLOWER TYPE	LEAF TYPE	LEAF ATTACHMENT
Flat	Regular	Simple	Alternate

ARIZONA MILKVETCH
Astragalus arizonicus

Family: Pea or Bean (Fabaceae)

Height: 6-20" (15-50 cm)

Flower: purplish pink, pea-like flowers in spike clusters, 4-6" (10-15 cm) long; each bloom, ½" (1 cm) long, has an erect, purplish pink upper petal (banner) with a large white spot with purplish pink veins

Leaf: feather-like, grayish green leaves, 1-4" (2.5-10 cm) long, are alternate and divided into 2-8 pairs of hairy narrow pointed leaflets

Fruit: erect tan pod, ½-1" (1-2.5 cm) long, is slender and flat; splits into 2 parts down the center

Bloom: Mar-May

Cycle/Origin: perennial; native

Zone/Habitat: desert scrub and grasslands at 2,500-4,500' (760-1,370 m); along roads, flats, mesas, rocky soils

Range: two-thirds of Arizona, in a wide band from the northwestern to southeastern parts of the state

Notes: This member of the Pea or Bean family has radiating, sprawling stems with erect flower spikes of relatively large, pea-like blossoms. The spikes rise above the silky-haired, grayish green foliage. A common weed in disturbed areas and in rocky soils throughout most of Arizona. It also occurs in New Mexico and northern Mexico. This plant is reported to have poisoned cattle, thus another common name, Arizona Locoweed.

CLUSTER TYPE	FLOWER TYPE	LEAF TYPE	LEAF ATTACHMENT	FRUIT
Spike	Irregular	Compound	Alternate	Pod

CORALBELLS
Heuchera sanguinea

Family: Saxifrage (Saxifragaceae)

Height: 12-24" (30-61 cm)

Flower: loose, dark pink-to-coral red clusters, 4-6" (10-15 cm) long, of bell-shaped flowers, dangling from thin stalks widely spaced along a slender fuzzy red stalk; each small blossom, ½" (1 cm) long, has 5 pointed petals around short yellow flower parts

Leaf: rounded heart-shaped basal leaves, 3" (7.5 cm) wide, are mottled cream on green, have toothed lobes and are on long stalks

Bloom: Mar-Oct

Cycle/Origin: perennial; native

Zone/Habitat: riparian deciduous, montane, subalpine at 4,000-8,500' (1,220-2,590 m); moist soils near shaded rocks, along rocky streams, coniferous forests

Range: southeastern corner of Arizona

Notes: This showy wildflower is only found in the southeastern corner of Arizona, in a small area of southwestern New Mexico and in northern Mexico. Has dark pink-to-red, bell-shaped flowers with flower parts that do not stick out, unlike the similar but paler Pink Coralbells (pg. 119), which has tiny, light pink, vase-shaped flowers with protruding flower parts. Coralbells forms a low mound, with flowers on stalks well above the foliage. It is often grown as a ground cover for its marbled cream and green leaves and for its attractive blooms.

CLUSTER TYPE	FLOWER TYPE	LEAF TYPE	LEAF ATTACHMENT
Spike	**Bell**	**Simple Lobed**	**Basal**

SCARLET BEEBLOSSOM
Gaura coccinea

Family: Evening-primrose (Onagraceae)

Height: 8-24" (20-61 cm)

Flower: spike cluster, 2-16" (5-40 cm) long, of flowers that turn overnight from white to pink to red; each blossom has 4 clawed petals and dangling red-tipped white male flower parts (anthers) backed by 4 downward-curving pointed pinkish green sepals

Leaf: narrow, lance-shaped, grayish green leaves, ½-3" (1-7.5 cm) long, have pointed tips and irregularly toothed or smooth edges; upper leaves smaller; several stems branching from base

Fruit: wrinkled diamond-shaped fruit, ½" (1 cm) long

Bloom: Apr-Sep

Cycle/Origin: perennial; native

Zone/Habitat: all life zones except subalpine at 2,000-8,000' (610-2,440 m); disturbed areas, among pines, old fields

Range: throughout, except the southwestern corner

Notes: This pretty, airy flower starts out almost white in the evening when it first opens, attracting moths that pollinate it that night. Turns pink by morning and red by afternoon. Flowers at the bottom of the spike open first. Spreads by underground stems, forming masses of plants. Can colonize in heavily grazed or disturbed sites in regions outside of its natural range. Navajo Indians drank a tea made from this plant to treat upset stomachs.

CLUSTER TYPE	FLOWER TYPE	LEAF TYPE	LEAF ATTACHMENT	FRUIT
Spike	Irregular	Simple	Alternate	Pod

NEW MEXICO CHECKER MALLOW
Sidalcea neomexicana

Family: Mallow (Malvaceae)

Height: 12-36" (30-91 cm)

Flower: deep pink or purple blossoms, 1-1½" (2.5-4 cm) wide, in a loose spike cluster, 6-12" (15-30 cm) long; each bloom has 5 blunted broad petals veined with white and has a green and white center

Leaf: fleshy fan-shaped basal leaves, 2-4" (5-10 cm) wide, on long stalks, have round-toothed edges; upper leaves are alternate and deeply divided into 5-6 irregular lobes

Bloom: Jun-Sep

Cycle/Origin: perennial; native

Zone/Habitat: riparian deciduous, montane, subalpine at 5,000-9,500' (1,525-2,895 m); meadows, along creeks, alkaline seeps and marshes, wet soils

Range: northern half of Arizona, except the northwestern corner; southeastern quarter of the state

Notes: Tolerant of salty water, this plant is also called Salt Spring Checkerbloom. However, it frequently occurs near fresh water in Arizona, such as along Walnut Creek in the Apache-Sitgreaves National Forests in the east central part of the state. Like others in the Mallow family, this flower's buds are twisted and flame-shaped, and the yellow flower parts are fused into a central column. The leaves were cooked and eaten as greens by American Indians.

CLUSTER TYPE	FLOWER TYPE	LEAF TYPE	LEAF TYPE	LEAF ATTACHMENT	LEAF ATTACHMENT
			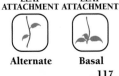		
Spike	Regular	Simple	Simple Lobed	Alternate	Basal

PINK CORALBELLS
Heuchera rubescens

Family: Saxifrage (Saxifragaceae)

Height: 5-12" (13-30 cm)

Flower: light pink spike clusters, 3-20" (7.5-50 cm) long, with many groups of vase-shaped flowers angling from thin stalks along a slender fuzzy stalk; each tiny blossom has 5 sticky, hairy, green-tipped sepals forming a vase holding 5 longer downward-curving petals and protruding flower parts

Leaf: long-stalked round basal leaves, ½-1½" (1-4 cm) wide, with 5-9 shallow toothed lobes; teeth are tipped with bristles

Bloom: May-Oct

Cycle/Origin: perennial; native

Zone/Habitat: montane and subalpine at 6,500-11,500' (1,980-3,510 m); dry to moist soils near shaded rocks, along rocky streams, coniferous forests

Range: northern half and southeastern corner of Arizona

Notes: The family name Saxifrage is from Latin words for "rock" and "break," referring to the habit of growing in rock outcroppings. This pretty, delicate flower makes an attractive addition to rock gardens in cool climates. The root contains alum, a drying agent that has been used to stop diarrhea, thus another name for this widespread species is Pink Alumroot. Limited to the southeastern corner of Arizona, the similar Coralbells (pg. 113) has larger, dark pink-to-red, bell-shaped flowers with flower parts that don't stick out.

CLUSTER TYPE	FLOWER TYPE	LEAF TYPE	LEAF ATTACHMENT
Spike	Tube	Simple Lobed	Basal

DESERT PENSTEMON
Penstemon pseudospectabilis

Family: Snapdragon (Scrophulariaceae)

Height: 1-4' (30-122 cm)

Flower: funnel-shaped, drooping, bright rosy pink flowers, ¾" (2 cm) long, in open spike clusters, 6-24" (15-61 cm) long; each sticky hairy bloom has bulge in lower half of tube, 3 rounded lower lobes bent downward, flat upper half with 2 rounded upright lobes; bearded, protruding, fifth male flower part

Leaf: stalkless, triangular, glossy leaves, 1-3½" (2.5-9 cm) long, toothed edges turned upward, fused together at their bases around smooth purplish green stems

Fruit: oval brown capsules, ½" (1 cm) long, held by persistent cup-shaped bracts on short stalks

Bloom: Feb-May

Cycle/Origin: perennial; native

Zone/Habitat: desert scrub, oak/pinyon pine/juniper woodlands at 2,500-7,000' (760-2,135 m); canyons, washes

Range: throughout

Notes: Similar in appearance to Parry Penstemon (pg. 123), but Desert Penstemon has broader tubular flowers that are darker pink and triangular leaves that are wider. Often cultivated in gardens, as it attracts hummingbirds. There are nearly 40 species of *Penstemon* in Arizona, a state known for its many species of hummingbirds and bumblebees, the two major pollinators of these wildflowers.

CLUSTER TYPE	FLOWER TYPE	LEAF TYPE	LEAF ATTACHMENT	LEAF ATTACHMENT	FRUIT
Spike	Tube	Simple	Opposite	Perfoliate	Pod

PARRY PENSTEMON
Penstemon parryi

Family: Snapdragon (Scrophulariaceae)

Height: 1½-4' (45-122 cm)

Flower: open spike cluster, 12-36" (30-91 cm) long, of pink tubular flowers; each flower, ½-¾" (1-2 cm) long, has fused petals forming a tube, flaring at the mouth; rounded 2-lobed upper and 3-lobed lower petals with darker pink middle vein; flowers in whorls about the almost leafless upper stem

Leaf: narrowly elliptical or spoon-shaped, bluish green leaves, 1½-6" (4-15 cm) long, are fleshy and stalkless, with smooth edges curling slightly upward; upper leaves much smaller

Bloom: Mar-Apr

Cycle/Origin: perennial; native

Zone/Habitat: desert scrub at 800-5,000' (245-1,525 m); canyons, flats, slopes, along washes

Range: southeastern Arizona and the area near Phoenix, often planted along highways and on medians

Notes: This pretty, pink wildflower occurs only in Arizona in the U.S., but it is very common at the lower elevations within its life zone. The seeds are a food source for birds such as Gambel's Quail. A favorite plant for desert landscaping and for butterfly and hummingbird gardens, as hummingbirds drink the nectar and pollinate the blooms. Often cultivated, growing readily from seed. Desert Cottontails eat the seedlings, so the young plants must be protected.

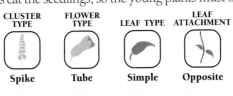

CLUSTER TYPE	FLOWER TYPE	LEAF TYPE	LEAF ATTACHMENT
Spike	Tube	Simple	Opposite

leaves

PALMER PENSTEMON
Penstemon palmeri

Family: Snapdragon (Scrophulariaceae)

Height: 5-6' (1.5-1.8 m)

Flower: fragrant, large-mouthed, pale pink-to-lilac flowers, 1½" (4 cm) long, in an open or a dense spike cluster, 3' (.9 m) long; each balloon-like bloom has 2 lobes flaring backward and 3 lobes bending downward; lobes are streaked with magenta

Leaf: triangular leathery leaves, 1-5" (2.5-13 cm) long, edges toothed or wavy, curving upward; smaller upper leaves joined at bases surrounding tall stems

Fruit: erect cup-shaped tan capsules, ½" (1 cm) long

Bloom: Mar-Sep

Cycle/Origin: perennial; native

Zone/Habitat: desert scrub, oak/pinyon pine/juniper woods and montane at 3,500-6,500' (1,065-1,980 m); along washes, slopes, among sagebrush, canyon floors

Range: northern half of Arizona, except the northeastern corner of the state

Notes: The tallest penstemon in the Southwest. Member of a group of penstemons with flowers designed for bee pollination, providing a landing platform and a swollen tube to accommodate the chubby bodies of bumblebees. The other group has narrow tubular red flowers to accommodate the needle-like bills of hummingbirds. Seeded in wildflower gardens for the showy, honey-scented blooms.

CLUSTER TYPE	FLOWER TYPE	LEAF TYPE	LEAF ATTACHMENT	LEAF ATTACHMENT	FRUIT

Spike	Tube	Simple	Opposite	Perfoliate	Pod

SMALL-FLOWERED MILKVETCH
Astragalus nuttallianus

Family: Pea or Bean (Fabaceae)

Height: 6-12" (15-30 cm)

Flower: small pea-like purple flower, ¼-½" (.6-1 cm) long, has an erect purple-to-blue upper petal (banner) with a large purple-veined white spot; 1-7 blooms grouped at end of the stems

Leaf: bright green leaves, 3" (7.5 cm) long, are feather-like and divided into 7-15 white-haired, narrowly oval leaflets; erect or trailing reddish stems

Fruit: smooth or hairy, curved slender pods, 1" (2.5 cm) long, are green and turn reddish when mature; pods are horizontal from the stem tips

Bloom: Feb-May

Cycle/Origin: annual; native

Zone/Habitat: desert scrub, grasslands, oak/pinyon pine/juniper woods at 100-4,000' (30-1,220 m); flats, mesas

Range: throughout

Notes: The most common of the annual milkvetch species in Arizona. Variable, it can grow in mats of sprawling stems sometimes less than an inch high or have erect stems up to a foot tall. Flower color also varies from white to light or neon blue, or from pink to purple. Can have smooth or hairy pods. Ranges from California east to Oklahoma and south to Mexico. Toxic to livestock, causing loss of weight, inability to control the hind legs or total paralysis.

FLOWER TYPE	LEAF TYPE	LEAF ATTACHMENT	FRUIT
Irregular	Compound	Alternate	Pod

BRISTLY NAMA
Nama hispidum

Family: Waterleaf (Hydrophyllaceae)

Height: 3-12" (7.5-30 cm)

Flower: upright tube flower, ½" (1 cm) wide, appears as a regular flower from above, but is actually tubular with 5 rounded spreading lobes; blooms are purple to reddish pink to pink-and-white, each with a pale yellow throat

Leaf: long and narrow to spoon-shaped leaves, ½-2" (1-5 cm) long, are grayish green, sticky, hairy, with blunt tips; the edges are partially rolled under; ends of sprawling, branching stems grow erectly

Bloom: Feb-Jun

Cycle/Origin: annual; native

Zone/Habitat: desert scrub below 5,000' (1,525 m); flats

Range: eastern two-thirds of Arizona

Notes: Bristly Nama is extremely common and abundant, forming mats that can carpet large areas of desert after heavy winter rains. In drought years, only a few plants producing a handful of flowers grow along washes, where some moisture is still available below the surface. This species is sometimes called Sandbells due to its preference for sandy soils and for the tubular flowers with widely spreading lobes, resembling upright bells. When cultivated and with added water, it makes a good, low-growing ground cover that blooms profusely throughout the summer.

FLOWER TYPE

Tube

LEAF TYPE

Simple

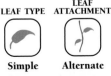

LEAF ATTACHMENT

Alternate

fruit

SNAPDRAGONVINE
Maurandella antirrhiniflora

Family: Snapdragon (Scrophulariaceae)

Height: 3-10' (.9-3 m); vine

Flower: snapdragon-like purple flower, ½-¾" (1-2 cm) long, has 2 upper erect lobes, 3 lower lobes, a triangular swollen white throat with a hairy bump lined with purple and a spotted tube; 5 pointed green sepals

Leaf: broad arrowhead-shaped leaves, ½-2" (1-5 cm) long, are dark to bright green, on a twining stem

Fruit: round green pod, ⅓" (.8 cm) wide, turning reddish brown, has a thread-like stem in middle; pod held by 5 pointed, persistent sepals that flare outward

Bloom: Mar-Sep

Cycle/Origin: perennial; native

Zone/Habitat: desert scrub, oak/pinyon pine/juniper woodlands at 1,500-6,000' (460-1,830 m); flats, slopes

Range: throughout Arizona, except the northeastern corner

Notes: This delicate-looking vine is often cultivated in Arizona for its showy, small flowers, which can be blue or reddish pink. Snapdragonvine has ivy-like leaves and grows well when planted in a pot with a trellis. A food plant for Common Buckeye butterfly caterpillars, thus it is also planted in butterfly gardens. Usually deciduous, dying off in winter and growing from the root in spring. However, it is semi-evergreen in some protected habitats.

FLOWER TYPE	LEAF TYPE	LEAF ATTACHMENT	FRUIT
Tube	Simple	Alternate	Pod

BROWN-PLUMED WIRE LETTUCE
Stephanomeria pauciflora

Family: Aster (Asteraceae)

Height: 8-20" (20-50 cm); shrub

Flower: pale lavender-to-pink flower head, ¾" (2 cm) wide, with 5 strap-like petals (ray flowers) with 4 notches at the tips around 5 lavender and white male flower parts (stamens)

Leaf: basal, narrowly lance-shaped, bluish green leaves, 1-3" (2.5-7.5 cm) long, with a white midrib and sharp lobes; basal leaves wither before the plant flowers; narrow unlobed stem leaves are tiny; up to 5 wiry, bluish green, multi-branching stems

Bloom: year-round

Cycle/Origin: perennial; native

Zone/Habitat: desert scrub, grasslands, oak/pinyon pine/juniper woods at 150-7,000' (50-2,135 m); along canyon walls, flats, slopes, along washes

Range: throughout Arizona, except the southwestern corner of the state

Notes: The basal rosette of this common aster dies before the plant blooms, and the twisting and branching stems form an open rounded shrub with few flowers, thus the plant is often overlooked. Named "Brown-plumed" for the feathery brown bristles on its fruit. "Wire" refers to the wiry, almost leafless, bluish green stems. The blooms of the other seven species of wire lettuce in Arizona have more petals.

FLOWER TYPE	LEAF TYPE	LEAF TYPE	LEAF ATTACHMENT	LEAF ATTACHMENT
Regular	Simple	Simple Lobed	Alternate	Basal

WANDERER VIOLET
Viola nephrophylla

Family: Violet (Violaceae)

Height: 2-12" (5-30 cm)

Flower: unusual nodding, deep violet flower, ½-1" (1-2.5 cm) long, has 5 petals with distinct blue or darker purple veins; 2 erect upper petals and 3 lower bearded petals have white bases; middle lower petal has a short sac-like spur

Leaf: wide, heart- or kidney-shaped basal leaves, 1-2½" (2.5-6 cm) long, are dark green above and purplish green below; round-toothed edges; on long stalks

Fruit: 3-valved elliptical capsule, ¼-½" (.6-1 cm) long

Bloom: Apr-Jul

Cycle/Origin: annual, perennial; native

Zone/Habitat: riparian deciduous, montane, subalpine at 5,000-9,500' (1,525-2,895 m); moist meadows, canyons, seeps, mountain slopes, along streams

Range: eastern two-thirds of Arizona

Notes: A stemless, low-growing violet whose smooth leafstalks and leafless flower stalks arise directly from underground stems. Early settlers made a jelly from the flowers and a tea that was used to treat headaches and sore throats. The leaves are very high in vitamins A and C. Grows only in moist places, thus it is often called Northern Bog Violet. Widespread throughout the United States, except for the southeastern states. Also found in the boreal forests of Canada.

FLOWER TYPE	LEAF TYPE	LEAF ATTACHMENT	FRUIT
Irregular	Simple	Basal	Pod

fruit

SILVERLEAF NIGHTSHADE
Solanum elaeagnifolium

Family: Nightshade (Solanaceae)

Height: 1-4' (30-122 cm)

Flower: loose groups of star-shaped purple (sometimes white) flowers; each flower, ¾-1½" (2-4 cm) wide, has 5 long triangular fused petals that are wrinkled and thin with wavy edges and surround the bright yellow protruding flower parts

Leaf: narrowly lance-shaped, greenish gray leaves, 1-6" (2.5-15 cm) long, with wavy margins and orange spines on veins below; long straight thorns on stems

Fruit: round berry-like fruit, ⅓-⅔" (.8-1.6 cm) wide, is smooth and hard; mottled green, turning orangish yellow when ripe; dangles from thorny stalk

Bloom: May-Oct

Cycle/Origin: perennial; native

Zone/Habitat: desert scrub and grasslands at 1,000-5,000' (305-1,525 m); abandoned fields, disturbed soils

Range: throughout

Notes: The grayish cast to the stems and leaves is from the covering of dense, star-shaped hairs. An invasive weed toxic to livestock. Spreads by deep underground stems, forming colonies that are hard to eradicate. The plant, which contains a digestive enzyme, was combined with animal brain tissue and used to tan hides. Pima Indians used the crushed fruit to curdle milk when making cheese.

FLOWER TYPE	LEAF TYPE	LEAF ATTACHMENT	FRUIT
Regular	Simple	Alternate	Berry

WILD HYACINTH
Dichelostemma capitatum

Family: Lily (Liliaceae)

Height: 6-30" (15-76 cm)

Flower: loose group of 2-15 flowers atop a leafless stalk; each funnel-shaped flower, 1" (2.5 cm) wide, is bluish or pinkish purple and has 6 partially fused petals with pointed lobes flaring outward

Leaf: basal leaves, 4-27½" (10-70 cm) long, are narrow and grass-like; only 2-3 leaves rise from the bulb; leaves often dry up before the plant flowers

Bloom: Feb-May

Cycle/Origin: perennial; native

Zone/Habitat: desert scrub, grasslands, oak woodlands, montane below 7,000' (2,135 m); flats, rocky slopes

Range: two-thirds of Arizona, in a wide band from the northwestern to southeastern parts of the state

Notes: Species name *capitatum* means "head-like," referring to the group of flowers that tops the leafless, fleshy flower stalk. The number of flowers in the group varies from 2-5 (sometimes as many as 15), depending on the variety. Often found blooming abundantly in areas cleared by fire, thriving due to the increased nutrients in the soil. American Indians dug up the bulbs, which taste similar to new potatoes, and ate them raw or cooked. Wild Hyacinth grows only in the western United States, ranging north to Oregon and east to New Mexico.

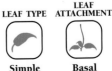

FLOWER TYPE	LEAF TYPE	LEAF ATTACHMENT
Tube	Simple	Basal

PLEATED GENTIAN
Gentiana affinis

Family: Gentian (Gentianaceae)

Height: 4-16" (10-40 cm)

Flower: 5-10 urn-shaped, violet-to-bluish purple flowers, 1-1½" (2.5-4 cm) long, crowded at top of stalk; each bloom is held by long pointed green bracts, has 5 petals that are dull bluish purple below and joined by a membrane between each petal

Leaf: rough, lance-shaped to elliptical leaves, ½-1½" (1-4 cm) long; pairs of leaves evenly spaced along erect or sprawling, burgundy-colored stems; the middle pairs are the longest

Bloom: Aug-Oct

Cycle/Origin: perennial; native

Zone/Habitat: montane and subalpine at 7,500-9,500' (2,285-2,895 m); meadows, along streams and springs, damp soils

Range: eastern half of Arizona

Notes: The genus *Gentiana* is named for King Gentius of ancient Illyria. "Pleated" in the common name is for the inward-folding membrane that joins the petals. Grows scattered in dense clusters of as many as a dozen plants in wet meadows and is sometimes called Marsh Gentian. Cultivated in rock gardens with damp areas where the sprawling stems can dangle over and be supported by stones. This wildflower can be seen on the famous Mount Baldy Trail in the White Mountains of east central Arizona.

FLOWER
TYPE

LEAF TYPE

LEAF
ATTACHMENT

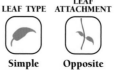

Tube

Simple

Opposite

TANSYLEAF TANSY-ASTER
Machaeranthera tanacetifolia

Family: Aster (Asteraceae)

Height: 4-20" (10-50 cm)

Flower: bluish violet flower head, 1-2" (2.5-5 cm) wide, is daisy-like and has 12-40 narrow petals (ray flowers) surrounding a yellow center (disk flowers)

Leaf: oval feathery leaves, ⅓-4½" (.8-11 cm) long, are grayish green, alternately attached, sticky, hairy, and highly divided into opposite pairs of lobes; each lobe is tipped with bristly hairs; reddish green stems are also hairy

Bloom: Jun-Oct

Cycle/Origin: annual, biennial; native

Zone/Habitat: desert scrub, oak/pinyon pine/juniper woodlands at 1,000-7,000' (305-2,135 m); along streams or roads, among creosotebushes, in old fields or disturbed areas

Range: throughout, except the southwestern corner

Notes: There are 13 species of tansy-asters in the *Machaeranthera* genus in Arizona; most are recognizable by the spiny bristle at the tip of each leaf lobe. The Greek words *machaer* and *anthera* in the genus name refer to the sword shape of the tips of the male flower parts (anthers). This tansy-aster can be identified by its fern-like or feathery leaves. It is sometimes cultivated from seed for the many showy flowers.

FLOWER TYPE	LEAF TYPE	LEAF ATTACHMENT
		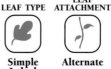
Composite	Simple Lobed	Alternate

143

HOARY TANSY-ASTER
Machaeranthera canescens

Family: Aster (Asteraceae)

Height: 2-4' (61-122 cm)

Flower: daisy-like, pinkish lavender flower head, 1-2" (2.5-5 cm) wide, has many narrow, blunt-tipped petals surrounding a yellow center; 4-8 overlapping rows of pointed sticky bracts, pale greenish white with green tips, curving outward

Leaf: narrow basal leaves, 1-4" (2.5-10 cm) long, with smooth margins; alternating stem leaves (cauline) are broader; upper stem leaves gradually reduced to tiny bracts; 1 to many stems are multi-branched

Bloom: Jun-Nov

Cycle/Origin: annual, perennial, biennial; native

Zone/Habitat: all life zones at 100-9,000' (30-2,745 m); disturbed ground, along roads and washes, riverbanks

Range: northern half of Arizona; the southernmost quarter, especially along the Santa Cruz River in Tucson

Notes: A highly variable aster, growing in many habitats and at most elevations in Arizona. This is a sprawling or erect plant with many branches and widely spaced leaves. It can have just a few scattered groups of flowers to many dense blooms topping the stems. Aptly named, "Hoary" is for the sometimes pale gray appearance of the velvety stems, and the species name *canescens* is Latin for "becoming gray." The seed heads are tan, fluffy and dandelion-like.

FLOWER TYPE	LEAF TYPE	LEAF ATTACHMENT	LEAF ATTACHMENT
Composite	Simple	Alternate	Basal

COLORADO FOUR O'CLOCK
Mirabilis multiflora

Family: Four O'clock (Nyctaginaceae)

Height: 16-27" (40-69 cm)

Flower: large, trumpet-shaped, purple-to-pink flowers, 1-3" (2.5-7.5 cm) long, centers sometimes dark, made up of fused petal-like sepals; held by papery cup of green bracts; in groups of 3-6 blooms

Leaf: short-stalked, round or oval leaves, 2-4" (5-10 cm) long, pointed or rounded tips, heart-shaped bases

Fruit: smooth or rough, oval brown pod, ½" (1 cm) long, sometimes with tan and brown ribs

Bloom: Apr-Sep

Cycle/Origin: perennial; native

Zone/Habitat: desert scrub, oak/pinyon pine/juniper woodlands and montane at 2,500-8,500' (760-2,590 m); open sandy areas, along roads, mesas

Range: throughout

Notes: *Mirabilis* means "wonderful" and *multiflora* is for "many flowers," referring to the multitude of spectacular blossoms on the mounded plants. The showy blooms open in late afternoon, emitting a musky fragrance nightly that attracts hawk moths, its main pollinator. Hawk moths have a long snout or proboscis that can reach the nectar at the bottom of the funnel-shaped flower. Navajo Indians boiled the blooms, using the mixture to dye wool a light brown or purple. This plant is found throughout the Southwest.

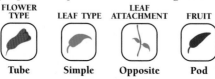

FLOWER TYPE	LEAF TYPE	LEAF ATTACHMENT	FRUIT
Tube	Simple	Opposite	Pod

TALL MORNING GLORY
Ipomoea purpurea

Family: Morning Glory (Convolvulaceae)

Height: 12-15' (3.7-4.6 m); vine

Flower: trumpet-shaped flower, 1½-2½" (4-6 cm) long, deep purple with lighter pinkish purple center; base of flower tightly enclosed by very hairy green calyx

Leaf: heart-shaped leaves, 2-5" (5-13 cm) long, on long stalks; twining red vine with long white hairs

Fruit: 3-parted spherical greenish pod, turning brown, ½" (1 cm) wide, flattened on each end

Bloom: Jul-Sep

Cycle/Origin: annual; non-native

Zone/Habitat: irrigated agricultural fields at low elevations; waste sites, roadsides, abandoned fields

Range: central Arizona; the eastern third and southern-most quarter of the state

Notes: This vine was introduced from Mexico and Central America to the United States and was planted in gardens. It has naturalized and spread widely throughout almost every state. Now an invasive weed, especially in the irrigated agricultural fields of Arizona. Many cultivated varieties with a wide range of flower colors (can be white, pink, blue or variegated) are available for planting and often escape to the wild. All parts of Tall Morning Glory are toxic, but the seeds, which contain a hallucinogenic compound, have been used medicinally.

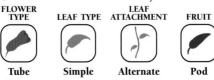

FLOWER TYPE	LEAF TYPE	LEAF ATTACHMENT	FRUIT
Tube	Simple	Alternate	Pod

fruit

ROCKY MOUNTAIN IRIS
Iris missouriensis

Family: Iris (Iridaceae)

Height: 8-20" (20-50 cm)

Flower: several large, bluish purple flowers, 2-4" (5-10 cm) wide, atop tall stiff stalks; 3 mostly solid-colored, erect petals; 3 drooping petal-like sepals heavily veined darker purple with beardless centers and white patches (throats) trimmed in yellow

Leaf: flattened grass-like blades, 6-20" (15-50 cm) long and ½" (1 cm) wide, light green with whitish bases

Fruit: wrinkled oblong green pod, 1½-2" (4-5 cm) long, with 6 obvious ridges, turns brown when mature

Bloom: May-Sep

Cycle/Origin: perennial; native

Zone/Habitat: montane and subalpine at 6,000-9,500' (1,830-2,895 m); moist meadows, aspen groves, ditches

Range: northern half of Arizona (except the northwestern corner) and the southeastern corner of the state

Notes: Commonly found throughout the western half of the United States and Canada, this is the only iris native to Arizona. The blooms and leaves resemble those of a garden iris; the flower color varies from dark blue to lavender to white. A paste of the ripe seeds was used by Shoshone and Paiute Indians to dress burns. The roots are poisonous and were ground up to make an arrow poison. Avoided by livestock, so it tends to overtake land that is heavily grazed.

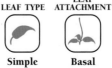

FLOWER TYPE	LEAF TYPE	LEAF ATTACHMENT	FRUIT
Irregular	Simple	Basal	Pod

BLUE PHACELIA
Phacelia distans

Family: Waterleaf (Hydrophyllaceae)

Height: 6-32" (15-80 cm); shrub

Flower: tightly coiled, hairy spike cluster, 1" (2.5 cm) long, of many bell-shaped, bluish purple flowers; each flower, ¼-½" (.6-1 cm) wide, has 5 rounded petals around a bluish purple center; flowers turn blue when wilted

Leaf: fern-like leaves, 1-4" (2.5-10 cm) long, are broadly lance-shaped, alternately attached and divided once or twice divided into pairs of finely hairy, toothed leaflets; branching reddish stem has sparse stiff hairs

Bloom: Feb-May

Cycle/Origin: annual, perennial; native

Zone/Habitat: desert scrub and interior chaparral at 1,000-4,000' (305-1,220 m); along washes, flats, rocky slopes

Range: throughout, except the northeastern corner

Notes: Also called Scorpionweed for the spike, which resembles the coiled segmented tail of a scorpion. However, the scorpion's tail curls upward, while the flower spike curls downward. The flowers vary in color from purple to blue to white and bloom from the bottom up on the spike. Although the more than 30 species of *Phacelia* in Arizona are hard to distinguish from each other, this one is easily identified by its pale purple flowers, weak straggly stems and its habit of growing under and getting tangled in other bushes.

CLUSTER TYPE	FLOWER TYPE	LEAF TYPE	LEAF TYPE	LEAF ATTACHMENT
Spike	Regular	Compound	Twice Compound	Alternate

153

DAKOTA MOCK VERVAIN
Glandularia bipinnatifida

Family: Verbena (Verbenaceae)

Height: 6-18" (15-45 cm)

Flower: violet-to-pink flat cluster, 1½" (4 cm) wide, of many small flowers, ½" (1 cm) wide; each flower looks like a gingerbread man with its 5 notched petals that are each a slightly differently shape

Leaf: dark green or bluish green leaves, 1½" (4 cm) long, are hairy and deeply cut into lobes, with edges curled under, oppositely attached to the hairy stem

Bloom: May-Sep

Cycle/Origin: annual, perennial; native

Zone/Habitat: grasslands, oak/pinyon pine/juniper woodlands, montane and subalpine at 5,000-10,000' (1,525-3,050 m); forest clearings, under trees, along roads

Range: throughout

Notes: The abundant nectar of the showy, long-blooming flowers attracts butterflies, thus this plant is frequently cultivated in butterfly or rock gardens. Dakota Mock Vervain is hardy and drought tolerant. Its sprawling stems result in mats covering large barren areas, making the plant a good choice for ground cover. In the wild in Arizona, it is often found carpeting the ground under evergreen oaks in the upper elevations of the grasslands or under pines in other life zones.

CLUSTER TYPE	FLOWER TYPE	LEAF TYPE	LEAF ATTACHMENT
Flat	Irregular	Simple Lobed	Opposite

155

NODDING ONION
Allium cernuum

Family: Lily (Liliaceae)

Height: 4-20" (10-50 cm)

Flower: drooping round cluster, 1-2" (2.5-5 cm) wide, of 8-35 bell-shaped lilac flowers (light pink or white when first open), whorled at the tip of the leafless flower stalk, which is bent like a shepherd's crook

Leaf: 3-5 grass-like leaves, 4-10" (10-25 cm) long, grow from the base of the plant and are flat or have a V-shaped channel

Fruit: 3-celled capsules held in nodding brown seed heads

Bloom: Jul-Oct

Cycle/Origin: perennial; native

Zone/Habitat: grasslands and montane at 5,000-8,500' (1,525-2,590 m); among grasses, openings in pine forests

Range: northeastern two-thirds and the southern edge of Arizona

Notes: This onion has the widest range of any of the numerous species in the genus *Allium*. It is native to North America, ranging northwest to British Columbia, northeast to New York and east to Georgia. One of the few onions grown for its flowers, although the edible bulb does taste like a common garden onion. The 2-5 bulbs per plant can be divided to grow new plants, or it can be grown from seed. Drought tolerant once established. Once used to treat croup, colic, fever, kidney stones or respiratory disorders.

CLUSTER TYPE	FLOWER TYPE	LEAF TYPE	LEAF ATTACHMENT	FRUIT
Round	Bell	Simple	Basal	Pod

WILD BERGAMOT
Monarda fistulosa

Family: Mint (Lamiaceae)

Height: 2-4' (61-122 cm)

Flower: many pale lavender flowers in a round cluster, 1-2" (2.5-5 cm) wide; each flower, 1" (2.5 cm) long, has 2 petals (lips) with the upper lip tipped with tuft of hairs; clusters sit atop the stems and branches

Leaf: lance-shaped leaves, 1-3" (2.5-7.5 cm) long, that taper to pointed tips and have coarse-toothed margins; each leaf is on a short leafstalk, oppositely attached to a square red stem

Bloom: Jun-Sep

Cycle/Origin: perennial; native

Zone/Habitat: riparian deciduous and montane at 5,000-8,000' (1,525-2,440 m); old fields, moist wooded slopes, forest edges, roadsides

Range: eastern two-thirds of Arizona

Notes: Also called Horsemint or Bee Balm, this is a tall single-stemmed plant of open areas and roadsides. Look for its square stems and oppositely attached leaves to help identify. Emits a strong scent when any part of the plant is rubbed or crushed. The fragrance of the blooms attracts many insects. "Bergamot" refers to a small citrus tree that produces a scent similar to that of this plant. Once used in folk medicine to make a mint tea to treat many respiratory and digestive ailments. Its oil is an essential flavoring in Earl Grey tea.

CLUSTER TYPE	FLOWER TYPE	LEAF TYPE	LEAF ATTACHMENT
Round	Irregular	Simple	Opposite

ALFALFA
Medicago sativa

Family: Pea or Bean (Fabaceae)

Height: 12-36" (30-91 cm)

Flower: tight spike cluster, 1-2" (2.5-5 cm) long, of deep purple-to-dark blue flowers (color can range to light blue); each small flower, ¼-⅓" (.6-.8 cm) long, has a 1 large upper petal and 3 smaller lower petals

Leaf: 3-parted and clover-like, 1-2" (2.5-5 cm) long, with sharp-toothed margins near tips

Fruit: downy green seedpod that twists into coils, turning nearly black with age

Bloom: Apr-Oct

Cycle/Origin: perennial; non-native

Zone/Habitat: all life zones at all elevations; agricultural areas, fields, along roads

Range: throughout

Notes: This deep-rooted plant is usually found in irrigated fields or along roads where it has escaped cultivation. Often planted by farmers in Arizona as a food crop for livestock and to improve soil fertility. Alfalfa hay is a favorite of horses and is often fed to them–sometimes to their detriment, as it contains a high percentage of protein that can lead to laminitis, a disease affecting the hooves. Prime host plant for Orange Sulphur butterfly caterpillars. Countless adult Orange Sulphurs hovering above an irrigated field of blooming alfalfa look like a swarm of dancing orange flowers.

CLUSTER TYPE	FLOWER TYPE	LEAF TYPE	LEAF ATTACHMENT	FRUIT
Spike	Irregular	Compound	Alternate	Pod

FEATHER PLUME
Dalea formosa

Family: Pea or Bean (Fabaceae)

Height: 18-36" (45-91 cm); shrub

Flower: short, deep violet-and-yellow spike cluster, 1-2" (2.5-5 cm) long, composed of 2-9 small pea-like purple flowers with the largest petal cream or yellow, surrounded by feathery sepals

Leaf: feather-like, grayish green leaves, ¼-½" (.6-1 cm) long, made up of 7-15 tiny narrow leaflets; leaves are semi-evergreen

Bloom: Mar-Jun, especially after rainfall

Cycle/Origin: perennial; native

Zone/Habitat: desert scrub and grasslands at 2,000-6,500' (610-1,980 m); rocky hillsides, mountains

Range: eastern three-quarters of Arizona

Notes: Sometimes called Feather Dalea, this hardy, low-growing shrub is a good choice for cultivation in the Southwest. It tolerates cold and heat, and it blooms profusely with little water. Don't overwater–the plant will become leggy. Pollinated by bees, but butterflies also visit the blossoms. Among the 36 species of prairie clover in Arizona, Feather Plume is the only one that forms a shrub with woody stems. It is especially common in the Chihuahuan Desert, part of which is located in southeastern Arizona, but Feather Plume is also found in New Mexico, Colorado, Utah and northern Mexico.

CLUSTER TYPE	FLOWER TYPE	LEAF TYPE	LEAF ATTACHMENT
		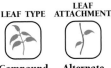	
Spike	Irregular	Compound	Alternate

GOODDING VERBENA
Glandularia gooddingii

Family: Verbena (Verbenaceae)

Height: 12-24" (30-61 cm)

Flower: violet-to-pink flat cluster, 1-3" (2.5-7.5 cm) wide, of many small flowers, ½" (1 cm) wide; each flower looks like a gingerbread man with its 5 notched, slightly different-shaped petals

Leaf: hairy arrowhead-shaped leaves, 1½" (4 cm) long, are dark grayish green, have toothed margins or are divided into lobes, are oppositely attached to the square stems

Bloom: Feb-Oct

Cycle/Origin: perennial; native

Zone/Habitat: desert scrub and riparian deciduous below 5,000' (1,525 m); slopes, mesas, roadsides, along washes

Range: throughout

Notes: Goodding Verbena is a desert plant, but it is dependent upon rainfall and also commonly grows near Arizona's rare desert streams. The showy flowers of this low-mounding plant attract butterflies, making it a favorite landscaping plant in the state. Also known as Southwestern Mock Vervain or Desert Verbena. Dakota Mock Vervain (pg. 155) is similar, but has leaves with deeply cut, thin lobes and is found at higher elevations than Goodding Verbena. Native to the American Southwest in lower elevation deserts, this plant is hardy in temperatures as low as 0°F (-18°C).

CLUSTER TYPE	FLOWER TYPE	LEAF TYPE	LEAF TYPE	LEAF ATTACHMENT
Flat	Irregular	Simple	Simple Lobed	Opposite

DESERT SAND VERBENA
Abronia villosa

Family: Four O'clock (Nyctaginaceae)

Height: 1-6' (.3-1.8 m)

Flower: round, deep purple-to-pink clusters, 1-3" (2.5-7.5 cm) wide, made up of 15-35 small tubular flowers of fused petal-like sepals flaring widely into 5 heart-shaped, purple or pink lobes with white bases; on erect, hairy, reddish flower stalks

Leaf: hairy, triangular to oval, grayish green leaves, ½-4" (1-10 cm) long, are on stalks and feel moist and sticky to the touch

Fruit: rounded triangular brown pod, ½" (1 cm) long, has wrinkled skin and is spongy inside

Bloom: Feb-Jul

Cycle/Origin: annual; native

Zone/Habitat: desert scrub below 3,000' (915 m); along roads, flats, dunes, sandy soils

Range: southwestern quarter of Arizona and the north-western corner of the state

Notes: This bright wildflower has many reddish multi-branching stems that sprawl across the ground. Forms large loose mats of hairy succulent foliage with blooms atop upright flower stalks. Often found with Dune Evening-primrose (pg. 247), especially after heavy winter rains, when these species carpet the open desert. *Villosa* means "hairy," referring to the stems, leaves and blossoms.

CLUSTER TYPE	FLOWER TYPE	LEAF TYPE	LEAF ATTACHMENT	FRUIT
Round	Tube	Simple	Opposite	Pod

GRASSLEAF PEA
Lathyrus graminifolius

Family: Pea or Bean (Fabaceae)

Height: 12-30" (30-76 cm); vine

Flower: spike clusters, 2-3" (5-7.5 cm) long, of 4-6 typical pea flowers, ¾" (2 cm) wide; flowers are pinkish lavender and white, and bloom along 1 side of stalk

Leaf: alternately attached leaves, 2-3" (5-7.5 cm) long, divided into 3-4 opposite pairs of narrow grass-like leaflets, 2-3" (5-7.5 cm) long; each leaflet has a smooth margin; each end (terminal) leaflet is modified into a clinging forked tendril

Fruit: green pod, turning tan, 5" (13 cm) long, has a typical pea pod shape

Bloom: May-Sep

Cycle/Origin: perennial; native

Zone/Habitat: grasslands and montane at 4,000-9,000' (1,220-2,745 m); forest clearings, slopes, gulches

Range: throughout Arizona, except the far western edge

Notes: The wild peas in this genus are weak-stemmed vines that climb up on other plants by taking hold with forked tendrils. Of the seven species of *Lathyrus* in Arizona, this has the narrowest grass-like blades, thus the name "Grassleaf." Its blossoms resemble those of the common garden pea. Like other members of the Pea or Bean family, its roots fix nitrogen into the soil, improving soil fertility.

CLUSTER TYPE	FLOWER TYPE	LEAF TYPE	LEAF ATTACHMENT	FRUIT
Spike	Irregular	Compound	Alternate	Pod

ROCKY MOUNTAIN BEE PLANT
Cleome serrulata

Family: Caper (Capparaceae)

Height: 1-4' (30-122 cm)

Flower: dense, fuzzy-looking, purple or pink spike clusters, 2-3" (5-10 cm) long, made of dozens of small flowers; each blossom, ½" (1 cm) long, has 8 petals and petal-like sepals and long protruding flower parts

Leaf: lower leaves are dull green, long stalked and divided into 3 oval leaflets, 1-3" (2.5-7.5 cm) long, with pointed tips and smooth or minutely toothed edges; simple leaves on upper part of waxy smooth stem

Fruit: curved bean-like green pod, 1-3" (2.5-7.5 cm) long, on a long stalk, turns brown, has 2 chambers containing several egg-shaped, mottled brown seeds

Bloom: Jun-Sep

Cycle/Origin: annual; native

Zone/Habitat: desert scrub, grasslands, oak/pinyon pine/juniper woods, 4,500-7,000' (1,370-2,135 m); flats, slopes

Range: northern half of Arizona

Notes: This was a well-known plant to Navajo and other American Indian tribes in the Southwest, who used it in a variety of ways. The leaves were cooked in meat stews or brewed into a tea to treat fevers and sore eyes. The seeds were made into a mush or bread. A black paint made from the plant decorated pottery. First collected by Lewis and Clark on their epic exploration of the American West.

CLUSTER TYPE	FLOWER TYPE	LEAF TYPE	LEAF TYPE	LEAF ATTACHMENT	FRUIT
Spike	Regular	Simple	Compound	Alternate	Pod

FRINGED TWINEVINE
Funastrum cynanchoides

Family: Milkweed (Asclepiadaceae)

Height: 8-40' (2.4-12.2 m); vine

Flower: pinkish purple or white round cluster, 1½-4" (4-10 cm) wide, of 15-25 star-shaped flowers; each flower, ½" (1 cm) wide, has 5 pointed, fuzzy-edged, pinkish purple and white petals and 5 sepals around a white protruding center made up of 5 inflated sacs

Leaf: variable-shaped leaves, ½-2½" (1-6 cm) long, with pointed or rounded tips and blunt or lobed bases

Fruit: narrow purplish green pod, turning brown, 1½-3½" (4-9 cm) long, is pointed at both ends, bulges in the middle and contains reddish brown seeds

Bloom: Apr-Oct

Cycle/Origin: perennial; native

Zone/Habitat: desert scrub and grasslands at 100-5,500' (30-1,675 m); on cacti, in ditches near cultivated fields

Range: throughout Arizona, except the northeastern corner

Notes: When broken or cut, the stems of this milkweed exude a white sap that smells foul and can irritate skin on contact. Grows from a large main root, which is hard to dig out; it will grow again from any small root piece left in the soil. Thus, although native, it can be an invasive weed in gardens and yards. The small seeds are attached to downy tufts that act as parachutes, which carry the seeds away on the wind, so it spreads readily from one area to another.

CLUSTER TYPE	FLOWER TYPE	LEAF TYPE	LEAF ATTACHMENT	FRUIT
Round	Regular	Simple	Opposite	Pod

OWL'S CLOVER
Castilleja exserta

Family: Snapdragon (Scrophulariaceae)

Height: 4-16" (10-40 cm)

Flower: dense, pinkish purple spike, 4-8" (10-20 cm) long, of many snapdragon-like flowers; each bloom, 1" (2.5 cm) long, has 2 rose-purple petals (lips); upper is beak-like and broad lower lip has white, yellow or darker purple spots; two-toned maroon and pinkish purple bracts

Leaf: fern-like, grayish green leaves, ½-2" (1-5 cm) long, are deeply divided into 5-9 thin lobes and covered with sticky fuzzy white hairs

Bloom: Mar-May

Cycle/Origin: annual; native

Zone/Habitat: desert scrub and grasslands at 1,500-4,500' (460-1,370 m); among creosotebushes, open flats, mesas

Range: parts of southern, central and western Arizona, covering about half of the state

Notes: This wildflower is especially common in Organ Pipe Cactus National Monument in southwestern Arizona. After good winter rains, masses of Owl's Clover mixed with other colorful annuals cover large areas of desert. This plant may be semiparasitic, getting nourishment from the roots of the other desert wildflowers. The seeds are stored (often by harvester ants) in the soil, where they stay dormant for years, until the next heavy winter rainfall. Frequently cultivated in Arizona.

CLUSTER TYPE
Spike

FLOWER TYPE
Irregular

LEAF TYPE
Simple Lobed

LEAF ATTACHMENT
Alternate

MacDougal Verbena
Verbena macdougalii

Family: Verbena (Verbenaceae)

Height: 24-36" (61-91 cm)

Flower: fuzzy, narrow, purple and green spike clusters, 16-18" (40-45 cm) long, of tiny densely-packed purple flowers blooming in rings of flowers from the top of the spike downward

Leaf: lance-shaped, dark green leaves, 3-4" (7.5-10 cm) long, are thick, softly hairy, sharply toothed and have prominent veins; the upper leaves are only slightly smaller than lower leaves

Bloom: Jun-Sep

Cycle/Origin: perennial; native

Zone/Habitat: montane at 6,000-8,500' (1,830-2,590 m); along roads, open areas, flats, grassy meadows, among ponderosa pines

Range: northern half and along the central southern border of Arizona

Notes: Extremely abundant along highways in northern Arizona. Unlike other species of *Verbena*, this stately plant has many tall showy flower spikes, and its flowers are pollinated by flies and bees rather than butterflies. The flower spikes turn maroon and become furry looking after blooming, then turn light brown and become rough when the tiny seedpods are ripe. Plant parts in this genus have been used as a diuretic, sedative or muscle relaxant.

CLUSTER TYPE	FLOWER TYPE	LEAF TYPE	LEAF ATTACHMENT	LEAF ATTACHMENT

Spike	Irregular	Simple	Opposite	Clasping

SCARLET CINQUEFOIL
Potentilla thurberi

Family: Rose (Rosaceae)

Height: 24-36" (61-91 cm)

Flower: groups of saucer-shaped, scarlet red flowers are on tall, almost leafless flower stalks; each flower, 1" (2.5 cm) wide, has 5 broadly heart-shaped petals with darker red bases and lighter red flower parts

Leaf: hand-shaped basal leaves, 2-4" (5-10 cm) wide, are dark green and divided into 5-7 finely toothed leaflets, ½-2" (1-5 cm) long, with silky hairs below and on long hairy stalks; much smaller stem leaves lack leafstalks and grow in whorls about the stem

Bloom: Jul-Oct

Cycle/Origin: perennial; native

Zone/Habitat: montane, subalpine at 6,000-9,000' (1,830-2,745 m); among coniferous trees, canyons, rich soils

Range: eastern half of Arizona

Notes: Plants in the genus *Potentilla* have five-fingered or palmate leaves, thus the common name "Cinquefoil," meaning "five leaves." A medium- to high-elevation plant in Arizona, it is found only in fertile soils among coniferous trees on mountains. Semi-trailing, it spreads somewhat like its close relative, Wild Strawberry (pg. 213), forming clumps and creating a hardy ground cover. The beautiful, velvet red flowers and dark green leaves make this an attractive addition to gardens with acid soils in cool climates.

FLOWER TYPE	LEAF TYPE	LEAF ATTACHMENT	LEAF ATTACHMENT
Regular	Palmate	Whorl	Basal

STAGHORN CHOLLA
Cylindropuntia versicolor

Family: Cactus (Cactaceae)

Height: 3-12' (.9-3.7 m)

Flower: cup-shaped, extremely variable-colored flower, 1" (2.5 cm) wide, has many sharp-tipped, spoon-shaped, overlapping petals and a yellow center; 1 to several flowers at the tips of the branches

Spines: clusters of stout, whitish or reddish brown spines, ¼-¾" (.6-2 cm) long; 6-11 spines per cluster, are unequal in length; tiny hair-like spines in a small crescent-shaped tuft next to each spine cluster

Fruit: cone-shaped green pod, 1-1½" (2.5-4 cm) long, is fleshy or leathery, spineless and contains tiny yellowish seeds; tinged red or purple when ripe

Bloom: Apr-Jun

Cycle/Origin: perennial; native

Zone/Habitat: desert scrub and grasslands at 2,000-4,500' (610-1,370 m); flats, rocky slopes, along washes

Range: south central Arizona, especially near Tucson

Notes: Aptly named *versicolor* for its flowers, which bloom in an astonishing variety of rich colors that range from greenish to yellow orange to red to purple, all with glowing yellow centers. An abundant tall cholla with an open antler- or candelabra-like appearance. Has erect stems branching frequently at diverse angles. Like most cacti, the dull green stems turn purple during drought or cold.

FLOWER TYPE

Regular

LEAF TYPE

Spines

FRUIT

Pod

CARDINAL CATCHFLY
Silene laciniata

Family: Pink (Caryophyllaceae)

Height: 12-27" (30-69 cm)

Flower: vivid red flowers, 1-1½" (2.5-4 cm) wide, have 5 deeply fringed petals; each bloom emerges from a tubular, hairy, ridged, reddish calyx, ¾" (2 cm) long

Leaf: lance- to spoon-shaped leaves, ½-6" (1-15 cm) long, are sticky and hairy; a few upper pairs of widely spaced, narrower and slightly shorter leaves

Fruit: cylindrical to egg-shaped tan capsule, ½" (1 cm) long, with reddish brown seeds

Bloom: Jul-Oct

Cycle/Origin: perennial; native

Zone/Habitat: interior chaparral, oak/pinyon pine/juniper woodlands, montane at 5,500-9,000' (1,675-2,745 m); grassy and brushy slopes

Range: eastern two-thirds of Arizona

Notes: Widely cultivated for its showy, serrated flowers, this long-blooming plant is easily grown from seed. If planted in early spring, it will bloom the same summer. Its nectar contains about 75 percent sucrose (ideal for attracting hummingbirds), and the plant is often pollinated by Anna's Hummingbirds. Many members of *Silene* are collectively referred to as catchflies, as the foliage is sticky enough to trap insects. In the wild, ranges from southern California to the southwestern corner of Texas (Big Bend area) and into Mexico.

FLOWER TYPE	LEAF TYPE	LEAF ATTACHMENT	FRUIT
Regular	Simple	Opposite	Pod

ARIZONA THISTLE
Cirsium arizonicum

Family: Aster (Asteraceae)

Height: 1-5' (30-152 cm)

Flower: as many as 100 red-to-orange (sometimes pink-to-lavender) flower heads per plant; each flower head, ⅝-2" (1.5-5 cm) long, is made up of thin tubular disk flowers held tightly by layers of spiny bracts with a central white line, arranged in a tight spiral

Leaf: highly variable leaves; oblong basal leaves, 1½-12" (4-30 cm) long, have spine-tipped teeth or lobes; stem leaves are usually clasping

Bloom: May-Oct

Cycle/Origin: perennial, biennial; native

Zone/Habitat: desert scrub and pinyon pine/juniper woodlands at 3,000-7,000' (915-2,135 m); foothills, canyons, pinewoods, along roads

Range: northern half and southernmost quarter of Arizona

Notes: Arizona Thistle is extremely variable in flower color and the shape of the leaves; the elevation at which it occurs is also variable. However, the flower always appears only partly open, since the bracts never allow it to spread into the typical wide disk shape of other thistle species. Attracts hummingbirds and bees, which pollinate the flowers. There are 17 species of thistle in Arizona, all of which produce seeds that are an important food source for birds, especially for Northern Cardinals and Lesser Goldfinches.

FLOWER TYPE	LEAF TYPE	LEAF TYPE	LEAF ATTACHMENT	LEAF ATTACHMENT
Composite	Simple	Simple Lobed	Alternate	Clasping

FIRECRACKERBUSH
Bouvardia ternifolia

Family: Madder (Rubiaceae)

Height: 2-4' (61-122 cm); shrub

Flower: slender, tubular, vermilion red flowers, 1-2" (2.5-5 cm) long, with petals flaring into 4 pointed lobes; in upright groups at the tips of the leafy branches

Leaf: lance-shaped, dark green leaves, 1-3" (2.5-7.5 cm) long, with pointed tips, grow in closely spaced whorls of 3 about the white-barked stem

Fruit: groups of small round green capsules, turning tan, ¼" (.6 cm) wide, are suspended on short stems and have many tiny brown seeds

Bloom: May-Oct

Cycle/Origin: perennial; native

Zone/Habitat: riparian deciduous at 3,000-9,000' (915-2,745 m); canyons, mountain slopes

Range: southeastern quarter of Arizona

Notes: In the United States, this mostly tropical plant is native only to southeastern Arizona, southern New Mexico and western Texas, but ranges far south into Mexico and Central America. Common along streams in canyons of Arizona, especially in Madera Canyon, a popular birding spot located south of Tucson that is famous for its many species of hummingbirds. As a cultivated shrub, it is well liked since it attracts hummingbirds to its honeysuckle-like flowers, which bloom profusely and continuously through the summer.

FLOWER TYPE	LEAF TYPE	LEAF ATTACHMENT	FRUIT
Tube	Simple	Whorl	Pod

BELOPERONE
Justicia californica

Family: Acanthus (Acanthaceae)

Height: 3-6' (.9-1.8 m); shrub

Flower: pairs of tubular, brick red flowers; each narrow flower, 2" (5 cm) long, has 5 fused petals with a notched upper lip and 3-lobed lower lip; 2 white-tipped male flower parts (anthers) project from tube

Leaf: hairy, pale green, oval leaves, ½-3" (1-7.5 cm) long, are evergreen, with pointed tips and wavy margins; oppositely attached to fuzzy stems

Fruit: club-shaped green pod, turning brown, ½" (1 cm) long, opens explosively to expel 2 seeds

Bloom: Mar-Jun

Cycle/Origin: perennial; native

Zone/Habitat: desert scrub and grasslands at 1,000-4,000' (305-1,220 m); slopes, flats, along washes, canyons, streambeds, planted in landscaping

Range: western third of Arizona

Notes: This plant is often cultivated to provide nectar for the 13-15 hummingbird species that live in or migrate through Arizona. Also called Hummingbirdbush or Chuparosa, which is Spanish for "hummingbird." Beloperone is a good plant for desert landscaping, tolerating heat and drought and recovering if frozen back to the ground. Leaves are present only when the plant is actively growing, dropping off during drought or cold.

FLOWER TYPE	LEAF TYPE	LEAF ATTACHMENT	FRUIT
Tube	Simple	Opposite	Pod

CARDINAL MONKEYFLOWER
Mimulus cardinalis

Family: Snapdragon (Scrophulariaceae)

Height: 10-32" (25-80 cm)

Flower: vivid red-to-orange tubular flower, 2-3" (5-7.5 cm) long, with 2 lips, yellow-streaked throat and protruding yellow flower parts; upper notched lip arches forward, lower lip has 3 notched lobes bent downward; a few blooms grouped atop stems

Leaf: stalkless, oval, dark green leaves, 1-3" (2.5-7.5 cm) long, fuzzy, sticky, with coarsely toothed edges and pointed tips; upper leaves clasp fleshy hairy stems

Fruit: oval, ridged, maroon-and-brown pod, ⅔" (1.6 cm) long, contains brown seeds

Bloom: Mar-Oct

Cycle/Origin: perennial; native

Zone/Habitat: riparian deciduous at 1,800-8,500' (550-2,590 m); wet seeps, along or in washes, shade to full sun

Range: throughout, except the southwestern corner

Notes: This moisture-loving wildflower is native throughout the far West from Washington to New Mexico, growing anywhere there is moist to boggy soil. Also grows well in gardens when planted near leaky faucets, birdbaths or fountains. Easily grown from seed and spreads widely by underground stems. The showy flowers are magnets for hummingbirds. Caterpillars of Checkerspot and Arizona's two species of Buckeye butterflies feed on the foliage.

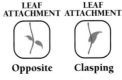

FLOWER TYPE	LEAF TYPE	LEAF ATTACHMENT	LEAF ATTACHMENT	FRUIT
Tube	Simple	Opposite	Clasping	Pod

FIRECRACKER PENSTEMON
Penstemon eatoni

Family: Snapdragon (Scrophulariaceae)

Height: 16-36" (40-91 cm)

Flower: eye-catching spike cluster, 1-1½" (2.5-4 cm) long, of scarlet red flowers; each flower is tubular with 5 equal lobes (lower lobe is curved downward); pairs of flowers grow along 1 side of flower stalk

Leaf: broadly lance-shaped or oval basal leaves, 1-3½" (2.5-9 cm) long, are dark green and leathery; stem leaves (cauline) are opposite and much smaller on upper stem

Bloom: Feb-Jun

Cycle/Origin: perennial; native

Zone/Habitat: desert scrub, pinyon/juniper woods, montane at 2,000-7,000' (610-2,135 m); among sagebrush or coniferous trees, along roads, riverbanks, slopes

Range: northern half and south central third of Arizona

Notes: Most penstemons have five male flower parts (stamens) and are commonly called "beardtongues" for their hairy fifth sterile stamen. However, the fifth stamen of Firecracker Penstemon has few or no hairs. The flowers provide a nectar source in early spring, attracting butterflies and hummingbirds. There are 13 species of colorful hummingbirds found regularly in Arizona, so planting and tending hummingbird gardens around homes is a popular pastime in the state. Also called Scarlet Bugler.

CLUSTER TYPE	FLOWER TYPE	LEAF TYPE	LEAF ATTACHMENT	LEAF ATTACHMENT
		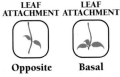		
Spike	Tube	Simple	Opposite	Basal

WOOLLY INDIAN PAINTBRUSH
Castilleja lanata

Family: Snapdragon (Scrophulariaceae)

Height: 12-36" (30-91 cm)

Flower: spike cluster, 1-4" (2.5-10 cm) long, of inconspicuous tubular red, yellow and green flowers, 1" (2.5 cm) long, interspersed among 3-lobed, woolly, leafy bracts; bracts are tipped with bright orangish red and are often mistaken for flower petals

Leaf: narrow pointed leaves, ½-2" (1-5 cm) long, are greenish gray and covered with dense white hairs; leaves alternate at widely spaced intervals

Fruit: small pod-like green container, ½" (1 cm) long

Bloom: Mar-Aug

Cycle/Origin: perennial; native

Zone/Habitat: desert scrub at 2,500-6,500' (760-1,980 m); flats

Range: southernmost quarter of Arizona

Notes: The leaves and stems of this perennial are covered with dense, intertwined, long white hairs, thus "Woolly" in the common name. The fresh or dried leaves were once used by the Zapotec Indians of Mexico when cooking beans or rice. Can be cultivated, but it is semiparasitic and needs to be planted near other species to absorb nutrients from their roots. Pollinated mainly by hummingbirds, which are attracted by the red bracts, but they get nectar from the tubular flowers. Ranges from California east to Texas and south into Mexico.

CLUSTER TYPE	FLOWER TYPE	LEAF TYPE	LEAF ATTACHMENT	FRUIT
Spike	Tube	Simple	Alternate	Pod

DESERT INDIAN PAINTBRUSH
Castilleja angustifolia

Family: Snapdragon (Scrophulariaceae)

Height: 6-16" (15-40 cm)

Flower: spike cluster, 2-6" (5-15 cm) long, of inconspicuous tubular green flowers, 1-1½" (2.5-4 cm) long, interspersed among fuzzy leafy bracts with 3-5 lobes; bracts are tipped with bright orangish red and are often mistaken for flower petals

Leaf: nearly clasping, grayish green-to-purplish leaves, 1-3" (2.5-7.5 cm) long, narrow and hairy, divided into up to 5 pairs of narrow spreading finger-like lobes

Fruit: small pod-like green container, ½" (1 cm) long

Bloom: Mar-Sep

Cycle/Origin: perennial; native

Zone/Habitat: desert scrub, interior chaparral, oak/pinyon pine/juniper woodlands, montane at 2,000-8,000' (610-2,440 m); among pines or sagebrush scrub

Range: northern two-thirds of Arizona

Notes: So named because each stem is topped with bright red, resembling a painter's brush. Legend has it that paintbrushes sprang up where an Indian discarded his brushes after painting a colorful desert sunset. Thought to be semiparasitic, its roots tap into those of other plants to gain nutrients. One of more than a dozen species of *Castilleja* in Arizona. Paintbrushes hybridize often, thus identifying a species can be difficult. Widespread throughout the West.

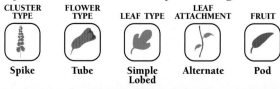

CLUSTER TYPE	FLOWER TYPE	LEAF TYPE	LEAF ATTACHMENT	FRUIT
Spike	Tube	Simple Lobed	Alternate	Pod

SCARLET HEDGE-NETTLE
Stachys coccinea

Family: Mint (Lamiaceae)

Height: 12-30" (30-76 cm)

Flower: scarlet red spike cluster, 6-18" (15-45 cm) long, of spaced whorls of 3-6 tubular flowers; each flower, ¾-1½" (2-4 cm) long, has 2 lips; upper lip is erect, while lower lip is broadly 3-lobed and dangling

Leaf: oval, dark green leaves, 3" (7.5 cm) long, are fuzzy, veined and toothed with pointed tips; evergreen at lower elevations, turning red in cold temperatures; square stems are covered with soft white hairs

Bloom: Mar-Oct

Cycle/Origin: perennial; native

Zone/Habitat: riparian deciduous at 1,500-8,000' (460-2,440 m); slopes, canyons, moist rich soils

Range: southern half and northeastern edge of Arizona, often planted next to birdbaths and garden fountains in Tucson and Phoenix

Notes: Easily grown in wet spots in gardens, where it blooms for months, this showy wildflower provides gorgeous color and attracts hummingbirds to its nectar. Like other members of the Mint family, it has hairy square stems, two-lipped tubular flowers and a minty fragrance. Requires moist soil and partial shade to thrive in Arizona, so it is most often found in riparian deciduous canyons in the wild. Also known as Texas Betony or Scarlet Sage.

CLUSTER TYPE	FLOWER TYPE	LEAF TYPE	LEAF ATTACHMENT
		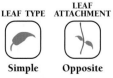	
Spike	Irregular	Simple	Opposite

BEARDLIP PENSTEMON
Penstemon barbatus

Family: Snapdragon (Scrophulariaceae)

Height: 1-4' (30-122 cm)

Flower: tall spike cluster, 8-18" (20-45 cm) long, of many tubular vermilion red flowers hanging along 1 side of stem; each narrow flower, 1-1½" (2.5-4 cm) long, has a protruding upper petal (lip), lower lip white-streaked at base and bent backward and downward

Leaf: grayish green basal leaves, 3-5" (7.5-13 cm) long, are sword-shaped with pointed tips and slightly wavy margins; stem leaves are opposite

Bloom: Jun-Oct

Cycle/Origin: perennial; native

Zone/Habitat: oak woodlands, montane and subalpine at 4,000-10,000' (1,220-3,050 m); commonly found along roads in northern Arizona, mountain meadows

Range: throughout, except the southwestern corner and scattered locations in southern half of Arizona

Notes: Genus name *Penstemon* is from the Greek words *pente* for "five" and *stemon* for "stamen," referring to the five male flower parts. This species has a yellow-haired tuft covering the whole lower lip, thus the name "Beardlip." It has a semi-evergreen basal rosette of leaves, although the flower stalks are deciduous. More than 40 species of *Penstemon* in Arizona, all with colorful and oddly-shaped tubular flowers pollinated almost exclusively by hummingbirds.

CLUSTER TYPE	FLOWER TYPE	LEAF TYPE	LEAF ATTACHMENT	LEAF ATTACHMENT
Spike	Tube	Simple	Opposite	Basal

SCARLET GILIA
Ipomopsis aggregata

Family: Phlox (Polemoniaceae)

Height: 16-30" (40-76 cm)

Flower: orangish red spike clusters, 10-24" (25-61 cm) long, of slim trumpet-shaped flowers, 1½" (4 cm) long; each bloom is red- or yellow-spotted inside, dangles from stem and has 5 long pointed petals that widely flare backward and long protruding flower parts; each blossom held by a small maroon calyx with tapering green-tipped lobes

Leaf: mostly basal, whitish green leaves, 1-2" (2.5-5 cm) long, are feather-like, woolly and divided into 9-11 short thin lobes

Bloom: May-Sep

Cycle/Origin: biennial; native

Zone/Habitat: oak/pinyon pine/juniper woods, montane at 5,000-9,000' (1.525-2,756 m); sunny slopes among pines

Range: northern half of and south central Arizona

Notes: *Aggregata* is Latin for "brought together," referring to the flowers clustering on the unbranched, erect, mostly leafless stems. The showy, odorless blooms are pollinated by hummingbirds. The leaves smell skunk-like when crushed. A basal rosette of leaves persists on the forest floor in winter its first year and withers before blooming in its second summer. Sometimes meadows are colored bright scarlet with large numbers of these blooming plants.

CLUSTER TYPE	FLOWER TYPE	LEAF TYPE	LEAF ATTACHMENT
Spike	Tube	Simple Lobed	Basal

CARDINALFLOWER
Lobelia cardinalis

Family: Bellflower (Campanulaceae)

Height: 2-5' (61-152 cm)

Flower: tall open spike cluster, 12-24" (30-61cm) long, of scarlet red flowers; each flower, 1½" (4 cm) wide, has 2 upper and 3 spreading lower petals that form a thin tube at its base; flowers alternate on the stem; lower flowers open before upper

Leaf: thin lance-shaped leaves, 2-6" (5-15 cm) long, with toothed margins and pointed tips; purplish green stem contains a milky sap

Bloom: Jun-Oct

Cycle/Origin: perennial; native

Zone/Habitat: riparian deciduous at 3,000-7,500' (915-2,285 m); along wetlands, meadows, wet soils

Range: throughout, except the southwestern corner

Notes: By far one of the most spectacular wildflowers of Arizona, Cardinalflower is found growing in small patches along streams and rivers. Can be grown in backyard oases near water. Its roots need to be wet, and its flowers must have partial shade as well as some sunlight. Not very successful at reproducing, perhaps because it can be pollinated only by hummingbirds. "Cardinal" refers to Roman Catholic cardinals, whose bright red robes resemble the scarlet red color of the flowers. Occasionally produces white or rose-colored blooms. All parts of the plant are poisonous.

CLUSTER TYPE	FLOWER TYPE	LEAF TYPE	LEAF ATTACHMENT
		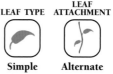	
Spike	**Irregular**	**Simple**	**Alternate**

WHITEMARGIN SANDMAT
Chamaesyce albomarginata

Family: Spurge (Euphorbiaceae)

Height: 8-16" (20-40 cm)

Flower: appears like a single flower, ⅛-¼" (.3-.6 cm) wide, but is actually a tiny, cup-shaped flower cluster; each bloom has 4 petal-like white bracts, each with a maroon pad at base, around protruding pink and green flower parts

Leaf: small, round or oblong, smooth, soft green leaves, ⅜" (.9 cm) long; sprawling stems have milky sap

Bloom: Feb-Nov

Cycle/Origin: perennial; native

Zone/Habitat: desert scrub, grasslands, interior chaparral, oak/pinyon pine/juniper woodlands, montane at 1,000-6,000' (305-1,830 m); forest openings

Range: throughout, except the southwestern corner

Notes: Plants in the Spurge family have colored petal-like bracts, not actual petals. The Christmas Poinsettia is a good example of this, with its red petal-like bracts. The tiny blooms of the widespread Whitemargin Sandmat are actually flower clusters with white bracts that look like single flowers. A pair of leaves and the associated flower cluster together measure less than the diameter of a penny. Although the blossoms are tiny, the plant is difficult to miss since one finds it underfoot everywhere, covering the ground in wide mats less than an inch tall. Also called Rattlesnakeweed.

FLOWER TYPE	LEAF TYPE	LEAF ATTACHMENT
		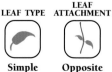
Irregular	Simple	Opposite

EMORY ROCK DAISY
Perityle emoryi

Family: Aster (Asteraceae)

Height: 2-24" (5-61 cm)

Flower: familiar round daisy flower head, ½-¾" (1-2 cm) wide, has 8-13 short oval white petals (ray flowers) with notched tips around a wide golden yellow center (disk flowers)

Leaf: triangular, dark green leaves, 1-4" (2.5-10 cm) long, are sticky, hairy, succulent and fragile, with edges irregularly deeply toothed or lobed

Bloom: Feb-Oct

Cycle/Origin: annual; native

Zone/Habitat: desert scrub below 3,000' (915 m); rocky slopes, canyons, arroyos, cracks in cliffs

Range: western two-thirds of Arizona

Notes: This happy-looking daisy with a round face is often seen sprouting from crevices on the sides of cliffs, flowering mostly in the spring, but sometimes year-round. Like other short-lived (ephemeral) desert wildflowers, the height and number of Emory Rock Daisies depend upon the amount of winter rainfall. In years with good winter rains, there are many of these wildflowers, and they grow as tall as 24 inches (61 cm). In drought years, only a few plants germinate from the many seeds stored in the soil and bloom when just a couple of inches tall.

FLOWER TYPE	LEAF TYPE	LEAF TYPE	LEAF ATTACHMENT
Composite	**Simple**	**Simple Lobed**	**Alternate**

TEXAS FALSE GARLIC
Nothoscordum texanum

Family: Lily (Liliaceae)

Height: 8-12" (20-30 cm)

Flower: star-shaped, yellowish white flowers, ¾" (2 cm) wide, have 6 similar-looking oval pointed sepals and petals with pink midline stripe below, surrounding a yellow center; 5-12 flowery-smelling blossoms on stalks branching from the top of stem

Leaf: 1-2 thread-like basal leaves, 3-6" (7.5-15 cm) long, are smooth-edged and wither before plant flowers

Bloom: Apr-May

Cycle/Origin: perennial; native

Zone/Habitat: desert scrub, grasslands, oak/pinyon pine/juniper woodlands at 4,000-6,000' (1,220-1,830 m); flats, slopes, shallow hard gravelly soils

Range: southeastern to central Arizona, ranging over half of the state

Notes: *Nothoscordum* means "false garlic," referring to the bulb from which it grows. This Lily family member has an onion-like appearance, but lacks any onion or garlic odor. Has three parts to its seed capsule, unlike the two-parted capsule of onion and garlic species in the genus *Allium*. Although common, it often goes unnoticed. An abundant spring wildflower after good winter rains, with masses of blooms carpeting desert flats. Can be seen east of the copper mining town of San Manuel, northwest of Tucson.

FLOWER TYPE

Regular

LEAF TYPE

Simple

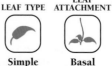

LEAF ATTACHMENT

Basal

fruit

WILD STRAWBERRY
Fragaria virginiana

Family: Rose (Roseaceae)

Height: 3-6" (7.5-15 cm)

Flower: groups of 2-10 white flowers; each flower, ½-1" (1-2.5 cm) wide, has 5 separated oval petals around a fuzzy yellow center

Leaf: whitish green basal leaves, 3-4" (7.5-10 cm) wide, made up of 3 leaflets; each leaflet, ¾" (2 cm) long, is coarsely toothed; leaves sit on a tall hairy stalk

Fruit: green berry, turning bright red, ¼-½" (.6-1 cm) wide

Bloom: Jun-Sep

Cycle/Origin: perennial; native

Habitat: montane, subalpine at 7,000-11,000' (2,135-3,355 m); meadows, coniferous forest edges, roadsides

Range: northern half and southeastern corner of Arizona

Notes: One of the two original species from which cultivated strawberries are derived and one of two wild strawberry species in Arizona. Flowers are larger than those of the garden variety of strawberry, which sometimes escapes into the wild. Often grows in large patches. It spreads primarily by underground runners, but also reproduces by seed. Its flowers and fruit are always on stalks separate from the leaves. Produces some of the sweetest of the wild berries. High in vitamin C, the berries can be eaten fresh or made into jam.

FLOWER TYPE	LEAF TYPE	LEAF ATTACHMENT	FRUIT
Regular	Compound	Basal	Berry

DESERT TOBACCO
Nicotiana obtusifolia

Family: Nightshade (Solanaceae)

Height: 8-32" (20-80 cm)

Flower: tubular, greenish white-to-cream flower, ½-1" (1-2.5 cm) long, with 5 blunted spreading lobes; held by hairy greenish calyx with 5 pointed lobes

Leaf: hairy, oval to lance-shaped leaves, ¾-4" (2-10 cm) long; lower leaves are wider at tips and with short stalks; upper leaves narrower, pointed at tips and clasping; hairy stems and leaves are both sticky

Fruit: oval green pod, turning brown, ⅓-½" (.8-1 cm) long, contains tiny brown seeds

Bloom: middle Mar-Nov

Cycle/Origin: annual, perennial, biennial; native

Zone/Habitat: desert scrub below 5,900' (1,800 m); along washes, rocky slopes, among creosotebushes

Range: throughout

Notes: The genus *Nicotiana* is named after Jean Nicot, the French ambassador to Portugal, who introduced tobacco to Europe in 1560. Desert Tobacco leaves were dried and smoked by early settlers and by American Indians, who used the plant for many medicinal purposes and ceremonial rituals. The foliage contains the poisonous alkaloids nicotine, which has been used in insecticides and anabasine, both of which are toxic to livestock.

FLOWER TYPE	LEAF TYPE	LEAF ATTACHMENT	FRUIT
Tube	Simple	Alternate	Pod

CANADA VIOLET
Viola canadensis

Family: Violet (Violaceae)

Height: 8-16" (20-40 cm)

Flower: typical violet-shaped white flower, ¾-1" (2-2.5 cm) wide, often tinged pink with age, sits on a slender purplish flower stalk; flowers stand above the leaves

Leaf: heart-shaped leaves, 1-3" (2.5-7.5 cm) wide, with pointed tips and bluntly toothed margins, on thin purplish stalks with sparse hairs

Bloom: Apr-Sep

Cycle/Origin: perennial; native

Zone/Habitat: montane and subalpine at 6,000-11,500' (1,830-3,510 m); coniferous forests, rich moist soils

Range: eastern three-quarters of Arizona, except the south central part of the state

Notes: One of the few "stalked" violets, the Canada Violet flower rises from a stalk that originates from a leaf attachment (axis), rather than the more typical basal flower stalk arrangement of most violets. It grows in patches from aboveground runners, called stolons, and is one of the few violets that has a fragrance. Found only on mountains in Arizona, but is widespread in the United States and ranges north into Canada. Canada Violet requires moist soils found in wet ditches along roads, near springs or in shady places under pine, spruce or fir trees.

FLOWER TYPE	LEAF TYPE	LEAF ATTACHMENT
Irregular	**Simple**	**Alternate**

FENDLER SANDWORT
Arenaria fendleri

Family: Pink (Caryophyllaceae)

Height: 3-7" (7.5-18 cm)

Flower: small groups of white flowers top long thin fuzzy stalks; each flower, 1" (2.5 cm) wide, has 5 separated oval petals; 5 pointed, grayish green bracts

Leaf: long, thread-like, dark green, mostly basal leaves, ½-2½" (1-6 cm) long, are sharply pointed and sticky; some leaves oppositely attached to stems

Bloom: Apr-Sep

Cycle/Origin: perennial; native

Zone/Habitat: montane and subalpine at 6,000-11,500' (1,830-3,510 m); at the bases of rock piles, coniferous forests, meadows

Range: northern half of Arizona and the mountains in the far southeastern part of the state

Notes: This perennial grows in compact, dark green mounds. Found in five states, from Arizona north to Wyoming and east to Texas, but it is most common in Arizona, Colorado and Utah. In northeastern Arizona, it is easy to find on slopes throughout the popular Canyon de Chelly National Monument, a unique park comprised entirely of tribal lands belonging to the Navajo Nation. People have occupied this scenic canyon continuously for 1,200 years. The Navajo historically used Fendler Sandwort to treat respiratory ailments.

FLOWER TYPE

Regular

LEAF TYPE

Simple

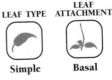
LEAF ATTACHMENT

Basal

CREAM CUP
Platystemon californicus

Family: Poppy (Papaveraceae)

Height: 4-12" (10-30 cm)

Flower: creamy white-to-pale yellow flower, 1" (2.5 cm) wide, has 6 oval flat petals surrounding a mounded cream center; flower atop a long leafless hairy stem

Leaf: grass-like, grayish green leaves, ½-3½" (1-9 cm) long, are hairy; the shaggy leaves are mostly on the lower part of the plant

Fruit: cylindrical green capsule, ⅔" (1.6 cm) long, turns brown and contains black seeds

Bloom: Mar-May

Cycle/Origin: annual; native

Zone/Habitat: desert scrub, grasslands, interior chaparral, oak woodlands at 1,500-4,500' (460-1,370 m); along washes, slopes, open grassy areas, moist soils

Range: two-thirds of Arizona, in a wide band from the northwestern to southeastern parts of the state

Notes: The stalks of the male flower parts (stamens) are flattened, thus the genus name *Platystemon*, which combines the Greek words *platus* for "broad" and *stemon* for "stamen." After good winter rains, this small multi-stemmed poppy often blooms among other desert annuals, such as the Arroyo Lupine (pg. 43) and California Poppy (pg. 341), but is often overlooked since its pale, creamy white color is overwhelmed by the bright colors of the other flowers.

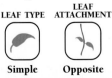

FLOWER TYPE	LEAF TYPE	LEAF ATTACHMENT	FRUIT
Regular	Simple	Opposite	Pod

RICHARDSON GERANIUM
Geranium richardsonii

Family: Geranium (Geraniaceae)

Height: 8-18" (20-45 cm)

Flower: white-to-pinkish flowers, 1" (2.5 cm) wide, have 5 rounded teardrop-shaped (sometimes drooping) petals streaked with lavender or pink veins, whitish-haired bases, a green center and upright flower parts

Leaf: maple-like, dark green leaves, 2-6" (5-15 cm) wide, are stalked, divided into 3-5 main diamond-shaped lobes; upper leaves are smaller

Fruit: long and narrow, erect pointed container, ¾" (2 cm) long, shaped like a crane's bill, contains 1 seed that is tipped with an elongated coiled tail

Bloom: Apr-Oct

Cycle/Origin: perennial; native

Zone/Habitat: riparian deciduous, montane, subalpine at 6,500-11,500' (1,980-3,510 m); meadows, moist soils

Range: northern half of Arizona, except the northwestern and southeastern corners of the state

Notes: One of the most common and longest-flowering plants along Arizona's mountain streams and hiking trails, such as the beautiful Oak Creek Canyon Trail near Sedona, Arizona. This low-growing perennial is found in coniferous forests wherever moist soils are present, sometimes nearly covering the forest floor. The dark green leaves turn red in the fall, making a striking carpet.

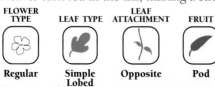

FLOWER TYPE	LEAF TYPE	LEAF ATTACHMENT	FRUIT
Regular	Simple Lobed	Opposite	Pod

DESERT PINCUSHION
Chaenactis stevioides

Family: Aster (Asteraceae)

Height: 2-12" (5-30 cm)

Flower: white-to-pinkish white flower head, 1" (2.5 cm) wide, of many tiny disk flowers that are larger at the outside rim; sticky, fuzzy, cone-shaped green bract

Leaf: elliptical basal leaves, ½-4½" (1-11 cm) long, larger leaves are divided once or twice into 4-8 pairs of short thin lobes; stem leaves gradually smaller going up stem; basal leaves wither before the plant flowers

Bloom: Mar-Jun

Cycle/Origin: annual; native

Zone/Habitat: desert scrub at 1,000-4,000' (305-1,220 m); shrublands among creosotebushes, flats, slopes

Range: throughout

Notes: Desert Pincushion is the most abundant spring flower in the upper Mojave Desert, and it is also very common in the Sonoran Desert and the rest of the Mojave. Also called Morning Bride. The central part of the flower head is composed of partially opened, yellowish or cream-colored disk flowers that turn white when fully open. Disk flowers around the outside edge of the flower cluster are often larger than central disk flowers. A look-alike species, Fremont Pincushion (*C. fremontii*) (not shown), is more abundant in the lower Mojave and northern Sonoran, has fewer stems, fewer flower heads per stem and paler green bracts than Desert Pincushion.

FLOWER TYPE	LEAF TYPE	LEAF ATTACHMENT	LEAF ATTACHMENT
Composite	Simple Lobed	Alternate	Basal

seed heads

APACHE PLUME
Fallugia paradoxa

Family: Rose (Rosaceae)

Height: 3-5' (.9-1.5 m); shrub

Flower: upright, rose-like white flower, 1-1½" (2.5-4 cm) wide, has 5 broad, slightly unequal-sized petals and a wide greenish yellow center of many long flower parts; borne singly or in small groups on long stalks

Leaf: clusters of small stiff leaves, ½" (1 cm) long, are dark green above and rusty below, divided into 3-7 rounded lobes; semi-evergreen, turning bronze and dropping during drought

Bloom: Apr-Oct

Cycle/Origin: perennial; native

Zone/Habitat: grasslands, oak/pinyon pine/juniper woodlands and montane at 3,000-8,000' (915-2,440 m); dry rocky slopes, arroyos, near seeps

Range: throughout Arizona, except the northeastern and southwestern corners of the state

Notes: A common, straggly, multi-stemmed shrub that is more noted for its tailed seeds than its flowers. The numerous seed heads are tipped by long, densely hairy, tail-like plumes that are 1-2 inches (2.5-5 cm) long (see inset). The feathery pink plumes make the plant appear topped with pompons. Named for the plumes, which resemble Apache Indian feather headdresses. The woody stems were once used for arrow shafts and brooms by American Indians.

FLOWER TYPE	LEAF TYPE	LEAF ATTACHMENT
Regular	Simple Lobed	Alternate

DESERT ZINNIA
Zinnia acerosa

Family: Aster (Asteraceae)

Height: 4-10" (10-25 cm); shrub

Flower: daisy-like flower head, 1-1½" (2.5-4 cm) wide, has 4-7 broadly oval, drooping, white or cream petals (ray flowers) with 3-lobed tips around a small protruding yellow center of 8-13 disk flowers

Leaf: rigid, smooth-edged, very narrowly lance-shaped or needle-like leaves, ⅓-¾" (.8-2 cm) long; leaves and stems are covered with sticky white glands; multi-branched stems are sparsely hairy and densely leafy

Bloom: Mar-Nov, but blooms best following winter and summer rains

Cycle/Origin: perennial; native

Zone/Habitat: desert scrub at 800-5,000' (245-1,525 m); flats among creosotebushes, mesas, calcium soils

Range: southern half of Arizona

Notes: A rounded or flat-topped, raggedly dense shrub with many small white flowers covering the surface of the mound. Aptly named Desert Zinnia for where it is found–in the deserts of the southern United States and northern Mexico. This pleasant, drought-tolerant perennial likes well-drained soils. Species name *acerosa* means "awl-shaped" and refers to the shape of the leaves. Foliage is smelly when crushed. Harvester ants collect the seeds and store them to eat later, coating them with antibiotic saliva to keep them from decaying.

FLOWER TYPE

Composite

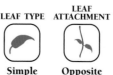

LEAF TYPE

Simple

LEAF ATTACHMENT

Opposite

BLACKFOOT DAISY
Melampodium leucanthum

Family: Aster (Asteraceae)

Height: 5-16" (13-40 cm)

Flower: daisy-like white flower head, 1-1½" (2.5-4 cm) wide, made up of 8-13 oval petals (ray flowers) with notched blunt tips around a yellow center; single flower head per stalk; many flower heads per plant

Leaf: grayish green leaves, ¾-1½" (2-4 cm) long, lance-shaped or narrowly oblong, have smooth margins or are sometimes divided into 2-6 shallow lobes; leaves oppositely attached to multi-branched stem

Bloom: Mar-Nov

Cycle/Origin: perennial; native

Zone/Habitat: desert scrub, grasslands, oak woodlands at 800-5,000' (360-1,525 m); along roads, slopes, flats, limestone soils

Range: throughout, except the southwestern corner

Notes: Cultivated in gardens and for erosion control in arid regions because of its hardiness and drought tolerance, this mounded evergreen perennial has many daisy-like, honey-scented flower heads per plant. Its long taproot allows it to reach water deep underground. "Black" in the common name is for the color the flower parts turn with age, and "foot" describes the developing seed, which looks like a black foot at the base of the yellow center. These seeds are food for birds in fall and winter.

FLOWER TYPE	LEAF TYPE	LEAF TYPE	LEAF ATTACHMENT
Composite	Simple	Simple Lobed	Opposite

SPREADING FLEABANE
Erigeron divergens

Family: Aster (Asteraceae)

Height: 5-18" (13-45 cm)

Flower: daisy-like, white-to-pinkish or lavender flower head, 1-1½" (2.5-4 cm) wide, of layers of 75-150 overlapping narrow petals surrounding a yellow center; up to 100 flower heads per plant

Leaf: narrowly spoon-shaped, bluish green basal leaves, ½-3" (1-7.5 cm) long; stem leaves are erect and fuzzy, getting progressively smaller up the stem

Bloom: Apr-Oct

Cycle/Origin: biennial; native

Zone/Habitat: desert scrub, grasslands, oak/pinyon pine woodlands, montane at 1,000-9,000' (305-2,745 m); disturbed areas, flats, among ponderosa pines

Range: throughout

Notes: A short plant with delicate-looking blooms, Spreading Fleabane is abundant in Arizona deserts. One of over 40 species of fleabane in the *Erigeron* genus in the state. Fleabanes are difficult to differentiate from one another due to variations in color, size and season of bloom. However, they are easily distinguished from other asters by the many narrow, overlapping ray flowers. While Spreading Fleabane is found in a wide range of elevations, the lavender-flowered Aspen Fleabane (*E. speciosus*) (not shown) can be seen mainly in mountain forests.

FLOWER TYPE	LEAF TYPE	LEAF TYPE	LEAF ATTACHMENT	LEAF ATTACHMENT
Composite	Simple	Simple Lobed	Alternate	Basal

DESERT CHICORY
Rafinesquia neomexicana

Family: Aster (Asteraceae)

Height: 4-24" (10-61 cm)

Flower: white flower head, 1-1½" (2.5-4 cm) wide, is tinged maroon below and yellow at the bases of the rectangular petals (ray flowers); has overlapping layers of blunt-tipped petals of varying lengths tipped with 5 small lobes; layers of pointed grayish green bracts

Leaf: grayish green leaves, 2-6" (5-15 cm) long, have pairs of thin lobes and are alternate; upper leaves are much smaller; hollow stems contain a milky sap

Bloom: middle Feb-Jul

Cycle/Origin: annual; native

Zone/Habitat: desert scrub at 200-3,000' (60-915 m); flats, mesas, among creosotebushes

Range: throughout Arizona, except the north central and southeastern parts of the state

Notes: This annual has frail flexible stems, so it grows under shrubs, using them for support and shade. Nonetheless, this is one of the more conspicuous flowers of the western deserts. Like the common carnation it resembles, the flower head has ray flowers only, lacking disk flowers; the centers are just yellow pigment at the base of the petals. The flower heads also look almost exactly like the blossoms of White Tackstem (*Calycoseris wrightii*) (not shown), but that species has sticky glands on its stems and bracts.

FLOWER TYPE

Composite

LEAF TYPE

Simple Lobed

LEAF ATTACHMENT

Alternate

STEMLESS TOWNSEND DAISY
Townsendia exscapa

Family: Aster (Asteraceae)

Height: 1-3" (2.5-7.5 cm)

Flower: white flower head, ¾-2" (2-5 cm) wide, has 20-40 long narrow white petals (ray flowers) and a yellow center (disk flowers); petals are pale pink below

Leaf: long and narrow or spoon-shaped, grayish-haired, dark green leaves, 1-3" (2.5-7.5 cm) long, in a dense basal rosette; evergreen, wintering as a small ball of leaves protecting the flower buds, which form in fall

Bloom: Mar-Aug

Cycle/Origin: perennial; native

Zone/Habitat: grasslands, oak/pinyon pine/juniper woodlands and montane at 4,500-7,500' (1,370-2,285 m); openings among ponderosa pines or oaks, rock crevices

Range: throughout, except the southwestern quarter

Notes: These very short perennials, which grow in leafy compact mounds a few inches wide, are aptly named *exscapa*, Latin for "without a stem." The large flower heads seem too big for the plant. A member of the Aster family, one of the largest plant families in the world. "Aster" means "star" in Greek, referring to the arrangement of the petals, radiating out from the center. Widespread throughout the western half of the United States. Can be found northwest of Walnut Canyon National Monument along the Arizona Trail, a hiking trail running the entire length of the state.

FLOWER TYPE
Composite

LEAF TYPE
Simple

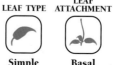
LEAF ATTACHMENT
Basal

DESERT ANEMONE
Anemone tuberosa

Family: Buttercup (Ranunculaceae)

Height: 5-16" (13-33 cm)

Flower: white-to-pale lavender (or pinkish) flowers, 1½" (4 cm) wide; each bloom lacks petals, but has 5-11 elliptical petal-like sepals around a fuzzy, green and pinkish lavender center; the sepals are finely hairy below; 1-5 flowers atop a single erect long stalk

Leaf: few basal frilly leaves, 2-4" (5-10 cm) long, on stalks and divided 1-2 times into stalkless lobed leaflets; 3 stem leaves in a whorl at midstem

Bloom: Feb-Mar

Cycle/Origin: perennial; native

Zone/Habitat: desert scrub at 2,500-5,000' (760-1,525 m); rocky slopes, cliff ledges, partial shade

Range: two-thirds of Arizona, in a wide band from the northwestern to southeastern parts of the state

Notes: Although it often goes unnoticed, this early spring wildflower has fairly large blossoms. The brown, woolly, cylindrical seed head, ½-1 inches (1-2.5 cm) long, produces seed-like fruits that are dispersed by the wind, thus it is sometimes called Windflower. The plant ranges in the southwestern United States from California to Texas and north to Utah and Nevada. It also occurs in Mexico. A good place to see Desert Anemone is along the Proctor Road Nature Trail in Madera Canyon, south of Tucson.

FLOWER TYPE	LEAF TYPE	LEAF TYPE	LEAF ATTACHMENT	LEAF ATTACHMENT
Regular	Compound	Twice Compound	Whorl	Basal

fruit

DEVIL'S CLAW
Proboscidea parviflora

Family: Sesame (Pedaliaceae)

Height: 1-3' (30-91 cm)

Flower: white and purple tubular flower, 1½" (4 cm) long, has a yellow line in throat and 2 lips divided into 5 lobes; 2 upper lobes, pointed and erect with purplish blotches; lower 3 lobes are slightly streaked inside with pink

Leaf: fuzzy, broadly triangular, long-stalked leaves, 2-6" (5-15 cm) wide, wrinkled with scalloped, toothed or lobed edges; hairy sticky reddish branches

Fruit: fuzzy curved okra-like pod, 7" (18 cm) long, dries and splits lengthwise into 2 curving sharp "claws"

Bloom: Apr-Oct

Cycle/Origin: annual; native

Zone/Habitat: desert scrub and grasslands at 1,000-5,000' (305-1,525 m); frequent near ancient Indian villages

Range: throughout Arizona, except the southwestern and northeastern corners of the state

Notes: Named for the split curved dry pods that resemble sharp claws. Pods catch on the legs of passing animals or on the heels of hikers, dispersing the seeds. American Indians of the Southwest grow this plant for the dry pod's fibers, which are used in basketry. The flowers and pods are often hidden below an umbrella of broad leaves. A yellow line in the flower's throat guides bees to the nectar.

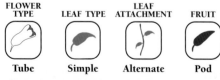

FLOWER TYPE	LEAF TYPE	LEAF ATTACHMENT	FRUIT
Tube	Simple	Alternate	Pod

FIELD BINDWEED
Convolvulus arvensis

Family: Morning Glory (Convolvulaceae)

Height: 1-6' (.3-1.8 m); vine

Flower: funnel-shaped white or pinkish white flower, 1-2" (2.5-5 cm) wide, has 5 petals fused together

Leaf: triangular or arrowhead-shaped, dark green leaves, 1-4" (2.5-10 cm) long, with smooth margins; leaves alternate along 1 side of the climbing, twisting stem

Bloom: May-Sep

Cycle/Origin: perennial; non-native, from Eurasia

Zone/Habitat: all life zones below 7,000' (2,135 m); old agricultural fields, along roads; usually creeps along the ground, but occasionally climbs on fences or shrubs

Range: throughout

Notes: Field Bindweed seems to prefer disturbed soils, old fields, abandoned lots in cities, and suburban lawns. Grows in large tangled mats, with white flowers that are sometimes slightly pink. This very invasive weed is difficult to eradicate due to its extensive network of roots and underground stems, which can grow as deep as 20 feet (6.1 m), and its seeds, which can live in the soil for as long as 50 years before germinating. Genus name *Convolvulus* comes from the Latin *convolvere*, or "to entwine," which accurately describes its growing habit. Lacking tendrils to grasp other plants, it twists its stems around host plants for support, seeking sunlight, a habit that provides its other common name, Possession Vine.

FLOWER TYPE — Tube

LEAF TYPE — Simple

LEAF ATTACHMENT — Alternate

DOUBTING MARIPOSA LILY
Calochortus ambiguus

Family: Lily (Liliaceae)

Height: 12-24" (30-61 cm)

Flower: tulip-shaped white flower, 2" (5 cm) wide, has 3 large petals, each with fringed blotch at the base; 3 pointed oval pinkish sepals; dark pink center

Leaf: grass-like basal leaves, 2-3" (5-7.5 cm) long, have a lengthwise groove; only a few smaller stem leaves; basal leaves wither before the plant blooms

Fruit: erect, narrowly oblong, brown capsule, 1½" (4 cm) long, 3-angled, has a pointed tip, contains flat seeds

Bloom: Apr-Aug

Cycle/Origin: perennial; native

Zone/Habitat: grasslands, interior chaparral, montane at 3,000-8,000' (915-2,440 m); slopes, open pine forests

Range: two-thirds of Arizona, in a wide band from the northwestern to southeastern corners of the state

Notes: This species is the most common of the five *Calochortus* lilies in Arizona. An erect bloom, it is also the most variable in flower color, ranging from white to purple and with variations in the dark purple markings on the bases of the petals; it may even lack the dark markings altogether. Genus name *Calochortus* means "beautiful grass" in Greek and refers to the narrow grass-like leaves. American Indians roasted and ate the bulbs of mariposa lilies.

FLOWER TYPE	LEAF TYPE	LEAF ATTACHMENT	FRUIT
Regular	Simple	Alternate	Pod

dried
stems

DUNE EVENING-PRIMROSE
Oenothera deltoides

Family: Evening-primrose (Onagraceae)

Height: ½-3½' (15-107 cm)

Flower: saucer-shaped white (fading to pink) flowers, 1½-3½" (4-9 cm) wide, have 4 broad heart-shaped petals around a yellow center; sweetly fragrant

Leaf: pointed lance-shaped leaves, 1-6" (2.5-15 cm) long, hairy above; branching spreading stems, outer stems turn upward

Fruit: curved and twisted, cylindrical tan pod, ¾-2½" (2-6 cm) long

Bloom: Feb-May

Cycle/Origin: annual, perennial; native

Zone/Habitat: desert scrub below 3,000' (915 m); flats, dunes, among creosotebushes, sandy soils

Range: southwestern and northwestern corners of Arizona

Notes: After good winter rains, this wildflower is easily seen on the Mohawk Dunes (east of Yuma, Arizona) blooming in masses with Desert Sand Verbena (pg. 167), covering large areas with color. As the plant dries, the outer stems curl upward and inward, forming a long-lasting structure reminiscent of old-fashioned wicker birdcages (see inset), thus also called Birdcage Evening-primrose. The species name *deltoides* is derived from the triangular-shaped Greek letter *delta* and refers to the shape of the petals.

FLOWER TYPE	LEAF TYPE	LEAF ATTACHMENT	FRUIT
Regular	Simple	Alternate	Pod

TUFTED EVENING-PRIMROSE
Oenothera caespitosa

Family: Evening-primrose (Onagraceae)

Height: 2-8" (5-20 cm)

Flower: white flower, turning pinkish white, 4" (10 cm) wide, with 4 wide heart-shaped petals and 4 long, thin, pointed, pink sepals that curve downward

Leaf: lance-shaped to narrowly elliptical basal leaves, 2-8" (5-20 cm) long, have irregular teeth or are lobed

Fruit: cylindrical brown capsule, turning woody, ½-3" (1-7.5 cm) long, is hairy, knobby and angled

Bloom: Apr-Sep

Cycle/Origin: perennial; native

Zone/Habitat: desert scrub, grasslands, interior chaparral and oak/pinyon pine/juniper woodlands at 3,000-7,500' (915-2,285 m); on rocky slopes, among ponderosa pines

Range: throughout

Notes: Like other Evening-primroses, this fragrant flower opens in late afternoon, blooms through the night and closes by the next morning. Pollinated by hawk moths, which are attracted by the white color and the scent of the flowers. It is evergreen in most habitats, but the foliage does turn red and drops off in cold conditions. A lovely addition to gardens in extremely dry habitats, as it likes well-drained soil and tolerates heat. Give it a little water weekly, and it will produce new blooms over a long period of time.

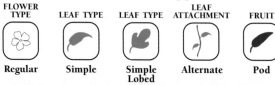

FLOWER TYPE	LEAF TYPE	LEAF TYPE	LEAF ATTACHMENT	FRUIT
Regular	Simple	Simple Lobed	Alternate	Pod

fruit

SOUTHWESTERN PRICKLY POPPY
Argemone pleiacantha

Family: Poppy (Papaveraceae)

Height: 1½-4' (45-122 cm)

Flower: slightly cupped white flowers with bright yellowish orange centers; each flower, 3-5" (7.5-13 cm) wide, has 4-6 wrinkled, paper-thin, overlapping petals

Leaf: lance-shaped, bluish green leaves, 2-8" (5-20 cm) long, have spine-tipped deep lobes; spiny stem

Fruit: oblong erect green pod, 1-2" (2.5-5 cm) long, turns brown; bumpy, spiny and has many tiny dark seeds

Bloom: middle Mar-Nov

Cycle/Origin: annual, perennial; native

Zone/Habitat: desert scrub, grasslands, oak/pinyon pine/juniper woodlands at 500-7,000' (150-2,135 m); mesas, along washes

Range: throughout

Notes: The white petals surrounding the orange center give rise to another common name for this plant, Cowboy's Fried Egg. Grows abundantly in overgrazed or otherwise disturbed soils such as along highways. The entire plant is poisonous due to the numerous toxic alkaloids it contains, although mourning doves do eat the seeds. The stem sap is yellow and foul smelling, but the flowers are fragrant and attract bees and moths. Interestingly, butterflies usually do not visit this poppy.

FLOWER TYPE	LEAF TYPE	LEAF ATTACHMENT	LEAF ATTACHMENT	FRUIT
Regular	Simple Lobed	Alternate	Clasping	Pod

fruit

SACRED DATURA
Datura wrightii

Family: Nightshade (Solanaceae)

Height: 1-5' (30-152 cm)

Flower: trumpet-shaped white (sometimes tinged with lavender) flower, 6-8" (15-20 cm) long, has 5 large fused petals with slightly wavy outer ends and a short spike at the middle edge of each petal

Leaf: arrowhead-shaped leaves, 1-10" (2.5-25 cm) long, are dark bluish green and have prominent veins

Fruit: globular prickly green pod, turns brown at maturity, 1½" (4 cm) wide

Bloom: Apr-Nov

Cycle/Origin: annual, perennial; native

Zone/Habitat: desert scrub at 100-6,500' (30-1,980 m); mesas, along roads and washes, disturbed areas

Range: throughout

Notes: The fragrant flowers of Sacred Datura, which are pollinated by hawk moths, open in the evening and wither a few hours after sunrise. All parts contain hallucinogenic compounds and are poisonous–just handling the plant can cause skin irritation. Daturas were important to American Indians, who used them for medicinal and ritual purposes, thus "Sacred" in the common name. Also called Sacred Thornapple for the seedpod, which resembles a spiny apple. One of five species in the *Datura* genus in Arizona.

FLOWER TYPE
Tube

LEAF TYPE
Simple

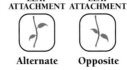
LEAF ATTACHMENT
Alternate

LEAF ATTACHMENT
Opposite

FRUIT
Pod

ROCKY MOUNTAIN PUSSYTOES
Antennaria parvifolia

Family: Aster (Asteraceae)

Height: 3-6" (7.5-15 cm)

Flower: loose round cluster, 1" (2.5 cm) wide, made up of 2-7 fuzzy white (sometimes pinkish) flower heads, ½" (1 cm) long; flower heads sit on top of a single fuzzy stem

Leaf: basal leaves, ½-1½" (1-4 cm) long, narrowly spoon-shaped and covered with white hairs, giving a fuzzy look; a few smaller pointed leaves on the stem

Bloom: May-Aug

Cycle/Origin: perennial; native

Zone/Habitat: montane and subalpine at 6,000-11,500' (1,830-3,510 m); openings among pines, sandy soils

Range: northeastern two-thirds and southeastern corner of Arizona

Notes: The bristly flower heads of this mountain aster resemble a cat's paw, hence the common name. A dense covering of hairs gives a grayish green color to the leaves and stems. Often grows to form a dense mat, pushing up through a layer of pine needles. It is an allelopathic plant, giving off chemicals that "poison" the soil for other plants, reducing competition for the limited moisture and sunlight on the forest floor. Rocky Mountain Pussytoes has fewer and larger blooms and is shorter than the other five species of pussytoes in Arizona.

CLUSTER TYPE	FLOWER TYPE	LEAF TYPE	LEAF ATTACHMENT	LEAF ATTACHMENT
Round	Composite	Simple	Alternate	Basal

BASTARD TOADFLAX
Comandra umbellata

Family: Sandalwood (Santalaceae)

Height: 6-16" (15-40 cm)

Flower: compact flat cluster, 1-2" (2.5-5 cm) wide, of 3-6 flowers; each star-shaped flower, ⅜" (.9 cm) wide, is greenish white to pinkish white, made of 4-6 petal-like sepals around a greenish yellow center

Leaf: many stalkless fleshy leaves, ¾-1½" (2-4 cm) wide, are narrowly oval, grayish green above and pale green below; multi-branched stem

Bloom: Apr-Aug

Cycle/Origin: perennial; native

Zone/Habitat: oak woodlands, montane at 4,000-9,000' (1,220-2,745 m); open fields, forest clearings, along roads, rock crevices, meadows

Range: throughout, except the southwestern corner

Notes: A semiparasitic plant, obtaining some of its nutrients from the roots of other plants. Its green leaves also use the sun to make some of its own food (photosynthesis). Forms colonies along horizontal underground roots. The greenish white flowers lack petals, instead displaying petal-like sepals. "Toad" in common plant names has been used to describe any plant that grows in the shade, but it also may come from the word "tod," which is a clump or tuft. Either explanation certainly describes this plant's flowering habit.

CLUSTER TYPE	FLOWER TYPE	LEAF TYPE	LEAF ATTACHMENT
Flat	Regular	Simple	Alternate

POISON MILKWEED
Asclepias subverticillata

Family: Milkweed (Asclepiadaceae)

Height: 1½-4' (45-122 cm)

Flower: flat cluster, 1-2" (2.5-5 cm) wide, of many small, odd-shaped, white-to-greenish white flowers, ½" (1 cm) wide; flower has 5 lower petals in a flat ring and 5 smaller upper petals raised above, looking like spokes of a wheel wagon; white central column

Leaf: thread-like, dark green leaves, 5" (13 cm) long, with rolled edges; in whorls of 3-5 leaves at stem joints

Fruit: erect slender flattened pod, 4" (10 cm) long

Bloom: May-Sep

Cycle/Origin: perennial; native

Zone/Habitat: grasslands and montane at 3,000-8,000' (915-2,440 m); among grasses, roadsides, along trails

Range: northern half and southeastern corner of Arizona

Notes: A very abundant plant in northern Arizona. This milkweed contains white sap poisonous to cows, sheep and horses; even its dried leaves accidentally bound in hay bales are lethal. Queen and Monarch butterfly caterpillars eat the toxic leaves with no ill effects, but they in turn become poisonous to birds if eaten. Conspicuous yellow, black and white stripes on these caterpillars warn potential predators to stay away. Also called Horsetail Milkweed for its segmented stems, which are like those of horsetails (grass-like sedges).

CLUSTER TYPE	FLOWER TYPE	LEAF TYPE	LEAF ATTACHMENT	FRUIT
Flat	Irregular	Simple	Whorl	Pod

ARIZONA POPCORNFLOWER
Plagiobothrys arizonicus

Family: Forget-me-not (Boraginaceae)

Height: 4-16" (10-40 cm)

Flower: coiled, hairy, white spike clusters, 1-2" (2.5-5 cm) long, made up of tiny tubular flowers with 5 rounded petals around a yellowish white center

Leaf: bristly haired, thick basal leaves, ½-2" (1-5 cm) long, oblong with pointed tips, edged with dark red along middle vein and edges below; a few smaller alternate stem leaves

Bloom: Mar-May

Cycle/Origin: annual; native

Zone/Habitat: desert scrub, grasslands, oak/pinyon pine/juniper woodlands below 5,000' (1,525 m); under oaks, among creosotebushes

Range: throughout Arizona, except the northeastern and southwestern corners of the state

Notes: The leaves contain a purple juice (used as a dye) that shows through at the middle vein and edges as a dark reddish color. The roots and stems also contain the juice, thus it is also called Bloodroot or Lipstickweed. The most widespread in Arizona, but also found throughout the Southwest and north to southwestern Utah. Can be seen in the nation's first protected archeological site, Casa Grande Ruins National Monument, south of Phoenix, which preserves an ancient Hohokam farming community and "Great House."

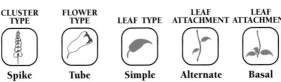

CLUSTER TYPE	FLOWER TYPE	LEAF TYPE	LEAF ATTACHMENT	LEAF ATTACHMENT
Spike	Tube	Simple	Alternate	Basal

SCRUFFY PRAIRIE CLOVER
Dalea albiflora

Family: Pea or Bean (Fabaceae)

Height: 12-24" (30-61 cm)

Flower: tiny pea-like white flowers in a cone-shaped dense spike cluster, 1-2½" (2.5-6 cm) long; each flower made up of 5 petals surrounding 10 long yellow male flower parts (stamens)

Leaf: narrow compound leaves, ½-1½" (1-4 cm) long, made up of 5-9 pairs of leaflets; leaves and stems are covered with tiny fuzzy white hairs

Bloom: Apr-Oct

Cycle/Origin: perennial; native

Zone/Habitat: grasslands, pinyon pine/juniper woodlands and montane at 3,500-7,500' (1,065-2,285 m); forest clearings, along roads and washes

Range: throughout, except the southwestern corner

Notes: Also called White-flowered Prairie Clover, the tiny flowers bloom from the bottom up on the spike. There are 36 species of prairie clover in the genus *Dalea* in Arizona. These members of the Pea or Bean family have the ability to fix nitrogen into the soil, thus enhancing soil fertility. Like many prairie plants, prairie clovers have roots that penetrate the soil deeply in search of water. The flowers attract many species of bees.

CLUSTER
TYPE

Spike

FLOWER
TYPE

Irregular

LEAF TYPE

Compound

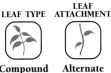

LEAF
ATTACHMENT

Alternate

ALPINE PENNY CRESS
Noccaea montana

Family: Mustard (Brassicaceae)

Height: 4-12" (10-30 cm)

Flower: cylindrical dense flower cluster, 1-3" (2.5-7.5 cm) long, of white to purplish pink flowers; each bloom, ⅜" (.9 cm) wide, has 4 spoon-shaped petals around green flower parts

Leaf: spoon-shaped basal leaves, ½-1" (1-2.5 cm) long, are toothed; oval succulent stem leaves clasp the unbranching stems at wide intervals

Fruit: stalked, heart-shaped, flattened, reddish green seedpod, ¼-½" (.6-1 cm) long, has a thread-like tip

Bloom: Feb-Aug

Cycle/Origin: perennial; native

Zone/Habitat: riparian deciduous, montane, subalpine at 4,000-11,500' (1,220-3,510 m); coniferous forests

Range: throughout, except the southwestern corner

Notes: This perennial begins flowering when only 1 inch (2.5 cm) tall, but the many unbranched flower stalks do grow taller and continue to bloom. Starts to bloom in early spring in low canyons and keeps flowering through the summer in the higher mountains. It often grows in large patches with few other kinds of wildflowers near it, providing a uniform-colored carpet of white or pink flowers. Often called Wild Candytuft.

CLUSTER TYPE	FLOWER TYPE	LEAF TYPE	LEAF ATTACHMENT	LEAF ATTACHMENT	FRUIT
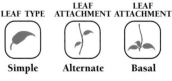					
Spike	Regular	Simple	Alternate	Basal	Pod

FRAGRANT SNAKEROOT
Ageratina herbacea

Family: Aster (Asteraceae)

Height: 12-24" (30-61 cm)

Flower: open flat cluster, 2" (5 cm) wide, of white flower heads, ⅜" (.9 cm) wide; each bloom is made up of tiny star-shaped tubular flowers (disk flowers) with long white male flower parts (stamens)

Leaf: triangular or lance-shaped, yellowish or grayish green leaves, 1-3" (2.5-7.5 cm) long, have toothed edges and prominent veins

Bloom: Jun-Oct

Cycle/Origin: perennial; native

Zone/Habitat: oak/pinyon pine/juniper woodlands, montane at 5,000-9,000' (1,525-2,745 m); openings in ponderosa pine forests, along rocky streams, slopes, ridges, arroyos

Range: throughout, except the southwestern corner

Notes: A common mountain perennial with white flower clusters that attract many species of butterflies and other insects. The whole plant is fragrant when dried. Woody underground stems (rhizomes), thought to resemble snakes, account for "Snakeroot" in the common name. Historically, the Navajo Indians made an infusion of the leaves and drank it as a tea or applied it as a lotion to treat fever and headaches.

CLUSTER TYPE	FLOWER TYPE	LEAF TYPE	LEAF ATTACHMENT
		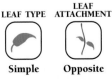	
Flat	Composite	Simple	Opposite

COMMON YARROW
Achillea millefolium

Family: Aster (Asteraceae)

Height: 12-36" (30-91 cm)

Flower: flat cluster, 2-4" (5-10 cm) wide, of 5-20 densely packed, white (sometimes pink) flower heads; each small flower head, 1/4" (.6 cm) wide, of 4-6 (usually 5) petals surrounding a tiny center

Leaf: fern-like, finely divided, feathery leaves, 4-6" (10-15 cm) long, have a strong aroma and become progressively smaller toward the top of the hairy stem; stalked lower and stalkless upper leaves

Bloom: Mar-Nov

Cycle/Origin: perennial; native

Zone/Habitat: all life zones above 4,500' (1,370 m); pine forest openings, fields, disturbed sites, along roads

Range: throughout

Notes: A common wildflower of open fields and along roads. A native of Eurasia as well as North America, Common Yarrows are probably native in Arizona since Zuni Indians in the state historically used the plant in rituals. Often confused with a type of fern because of its leaves. Grows in large clusters due to a horizontal underground stem. *Achillea* comes from the Greek legend that Achilles used the plant to treat bleeding wounds during the Trojan War. *Millefolium* means "thousand leaves," referring to the many divisions of the leaf, making one leaf look like many.

CLUSTER TYPE

Flat

FLOWER TYPE

Composite

LEAF TYPE

Simple Lobed

LEAF ATTACHMENT

Alternate

flower

fruit

SPIDER MILKWEED
Asclepias asperula

Family: Milkweed (Asclepiadaceae)

Height: 8-24" (20-61 cm)

Flower: round clusters, 3" (7.5 cm) wide, of greenish white flowers tinged with purple; each bloom, ½" (1 cm) wide, has 5 upward-curving petals and a 5-part crown of purple horns tipped with white

Leaf: narrow triangular leaves, 4-6" (10-15 cm) long, are dark green with a grayish middle vein and have pointed tips and wavy edges that curl upward

Fruit: stout curved conical pod, 6" (15 cm) long, is green with pink streaks and has deep lengthwise wrinkles and a pointed tip; contains flat brown seeds

Bloom: Apr-Aug

Cycle/Origin: perennial; native

Zone/Habitat: desert scrub, oak/pinyon pine/juniper woodlands, and montane at 3,000-9,000' (915-2,745 m); flats, slopes, along sandy washes, openings among trees

Range: throughout, except the southwestern corner

Notes: Pairs of conical pods resemble the curved horns of the Pronghorn Antelope, thus it is also called Antelope Horns. Inside the pod, teardrop-shaped seeds are in spiral layers around hair-like white fuzz that carry the seeds away on the wind. The foliage, which contains alkaloids, is eaten by Monarch butterfly caterpillars, rendering them and resulting butterflies poisonous to predators.

CLUSTER TYPE	FLOWER TYPE	LEAF TYPE	LEAF ATTACHMENT	FRUIT
Round	**Irregular**	**Simple**	**Alternate**	**Pod**

WOOLLY PLANTAIN
Plantago patagonica

Family: Plantain (Plantaginaceae)

Height: 2-10" (5-25 cm)

Flower: hairy greenish white spike cluster, 1-5" (2.5-13 cm) long, of tiny crowded flowers interspersed with white-haired pointed green bracts; each blossom has 4 translucent white-to-tan petals around a red center; 1-20 flower spikes per plant

Leaf: hairy, long, narrow basal leaves, 1-6" (2.5-15 cm) long, with pointed tips

Bloom: Feb-Jul

Cycle/Origin: annual; native

Zone/Habitat: grasslands, interior chaparral and oak/pinyon pine/juniper woodlands at 1,000-7,500' (305-2,285 m); along roads, mesas, slopes

Range: throughout, except the southwestern corner

Notes: Although the flowers of Woolly Plantain are inconspicuous, the flower spikes of this common small annual are noticeable when they grow in masses along highways. The whole plant is densely covered with woolly white hairs, but it looks greenish from a distance. American Indians curbed their appetites with a tea brewed from the plant and used it to treat headaches and diarrhea. It is sometimes called Indian Wheat because the seeds were once harvested for food. The seeds are also eaten by birds and small rodents. This plant is widespread across the United States.

CLUSTER TYPE	FLOWER TYPE	LEAF TYPE	LEAF ATTACHMENT
Spike	Regular	Simple	Basal

NARROWLEAF POPCORNFLOWER
Cryptantha spp.

Family: Forget-me-not (Boraginaceae)

Height: 3-18" (7.5-45 cm)

Flower: coiled spike cluster, 2-5" (5-13 cm) long, of tiny white flowers; each tubular flower made of 5 fused petals held by very fuzzy green bract

Leaf: narrowly lance-shaped or oblong basal leaves, ½-1½" (1-4 cm) long, are grayish green, opposite or alternate; leaves and stems densely covered with stiff bristly white hairs

Bloom: Feb-Jun

Cycle/Origin: annual; native

Zone/Habitat: 512-8,500' (160-2,591 m), from deserts to the pine belt

Range: all over Arizona

Notes: The flowers of the genus *Cryptantha* (Greek for "hidden flower") are very small. Often the 35 species in Arizona can only be distinguished from each other with a floral key and a microscope. One species, Desert Popcornflower (also called Narrowleaf Popcornflower) is widespread and abundant in the deserts. The slow-moving desert tortoises eat this very fuzzy plant. Although Popcornflowers (*Cryptantha* spp.) are in the same family and share their common name with the much less hairy Arizona Popcornflower (pg. 261), they are not closely related.

CLUSTER TYPE	FLOWER TYPE	LEAF TYPE	LEAF ATTACHMENT	LEAF ATTACHMENT
		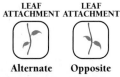		
Spike	Tube	Simple	Alternate	Opposite

fruit

FALSE SOLOMON'S SEAL
Maianthemum racemosum

Family: Lily (Liliaceae)

Height: 12-36" (30-91 cm)

Flower: spike cluster, 3-5" (7.5-13 cm) long, of tiny star-shaped white flowers, at end of single long arching stem; each flower, ⅛" (.3 cm) wide, has 3 petals and 3 petal-like sepals, giving the appearance of 6 petals

Leaf: stalkless elliptical leaves, 3-6" (7.5-15 cm) long, heavy parallel veining above, finely hairy below

Fruit: clusters of waxy green berries with red speckles; each berry, ¼" (.6 cm) wide, turns translucent red

Bloom: May-Jul

Cycle/Origin: perennial; native

Zone/Habitat: montane and subalpine at 6,000-10,000' (1,830-3,050 m); coniferous forests, moist soils

Range: northeastern third and southwestern corner of Arizona

Notes: The dense spike flower cluster at the end of the arching stem and the red berries are characteristic of this plant. Grows on forest floors from an elongated horizontal underground stem. Its waxy berries are not edible. A round scar on the stem (left after the stem has broken off) resembles the seal of King Solomon, hence the reference in the common name. Also called Solomon's Plume for the feather-like flower spike.

CLUSTER TYPE	FLOWER TYPE	LEAF TYPE	LEAF ATTACHMENT	FRUIT
Spike	Regular	Simple	Alternate	Berry

fruit

RED WHISKER CLAMMYWEED
Polanisia dodecandra

Family: Caper (Capparaceae)

Height: 12-36" (30-91 cm)

Flower: elongated flower clusters, 2-6" (5-15 cm) long, of frilly, pinkish white flowers; each bloom, ¾" (2 cm) wide, has 4 clawed petals notched at tips, many protruding pinkish purple flower parts

Leaf: stalked, dark green leaves, 2½-4" (6-10 cm) long, are clammy to the touch and divided into 3 fine-haired elliptical leaflets; upper leaves are smaller

Fruit: bean-like, reddish green pod, 1-3" (2.5-7.5 cm) long, is erect, flattened and fuzzy, turns tan

Bloom: May-Oct

Cycle/Origin: annual; native

Zone/Habitat: desert scrub at 1,000-6,500' (305-1,980 m); along roads and washes, disturbed areas, banks of streams

Range: wide band down the center of Arizona, from the northern to southern borders

Notes: The foliage of this sticky-haired annual has a rank resinous odor and so many glands on its surface that it feels chilly and moist, thus the name "Clammyweed." *Dodecandra* means "having 12 stamens" in Latin, referring to the long obvious flower parts. Often cultivated for the scentless airy flowers, it self-sows readily, filling in empty spots in the garden. Grows best in full sun.

CLUSTER TYPE	FLOWER TYPE	LEAF TYPE	LEAF ATTACHMENT	FRUIT
Round	Irregular	Palmate	Alternate	Pod

WESTERN WHITE CLEMATIS
Clematis ligusticifolia

Family: Buttercup (Ranunculaceae)

Height: 9-18' (2.7-5.5 m); vine

Flower: flat, dense, white or cream cluster, 3-8" (7.5-20 cm) wide, of 7-20 flowers, 1" (2.5 cm) wide; has 4 white petal-like sepals around erect white flower parts

Leaf: smooth, stalked, dark green leaves divided into 5-7 irregularly toothed or lobed leaflets that are 1-3½" (2.5-9 cm) long; leaves oppositely attached

Fruit: fuzzy ball-shaped green fruit, 1½-2" (4-5 cm) wide, contains a single seed with many long silky hairs; fruit bursts when ripe, releasing the fluff and seed

Bloom: May-Sep

Cycle/Origin: perennial; native

Zone/Habitat: interior chaparral, oak/pinyon pine/juniper woods, riparian deciduous, montane at 3,000-8,000' (915-2,440 m); climbing in trees, on fences, near seeps

Range: eastern two-thirds of Arizona

Notes: This woody vine forms dense clinging mats high in shrubs or trees. In the female plants, the flowers are followed by large white or yellow plumes of fluff and seeds, thus another common name, Old Man's Beard. This fluff makes excellent tinder for starting fires and has been used as insulation in footwear and to soak up moisture in babies' diapers. An extract made from the peppery leaves was once used by American Indians to treat colds and skin sores.

CLUSTER TYPE	FLOWER TYPE	LEAF TYPE	LEAF ATTACHMENT	FRUIT
Flat	Regular	Compound	Opposite	Pod

fruit

SHEPHERD'S PURSE
Capsella bursa-pastoris

Family: Mustard (Brassicaceae)

Height: 4-24" (10-61 cm)

Flower: very loose spike cluster, 3-10" (7.5-25 cm) long, of small white flowers, each ¼" (.6 cm) wide; flowers widely spaced along stem on horizontal stalks and densely packed at the top

Leaf: basal rosette of many oblong leaves, 2-4" (5-10 cm) long, are deeply lobed and finely toothed; a few narrower, lance-shaped stem leaves clasp the stem; both types have star-shaped hairs on the edges

Fruit: flattened heart-shaped green pod, turning tan, ¼" (.6 cm) long

Bloom: year-round

Cycle/Origin: annual; non-native, from Europe

Zone/Habitat: all life zones below 7,000' (2,135 m); in disturbed areas, roadsides, fields

Range: eastern three-quarters of Arizona

Notes: Considered an invasive weed, Shepherd's Purse is commonly found in every state. One of the earliest- and latest-flowering plants, wherever it occurs. Its heart-shaped seedpods are typical of all plants in the Mustard family and are edible. The basal leaves, which grow before the flower stalks appear, can be eaten raw in salads or cooked as greens. Related to the common garden cabbage.

CLUSTER TYPE	FLOWER TYPE	LEAF TYPE	LEAF ATTACHMENT	LEAF ATTACHMENT	FRUIT
				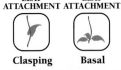	
Spike	Regular	Simple Lobed	Clasping	Basal	Pod

DESERT LILY
Hesperocallis undulata

Family: Lily (Liliaceae)

Height: 1-4' (30-122 cm)

Flower: loose spike cluster, 4-12" (10-30 cm) long, of large trumpet-shaped white flowers, 3" (7.5 cm) long; each bloom has 6 waxy long oval petals with a greenish silver streak on the back, flaring widely around protruding yellow-tipped flowers parts

Leaf: bluish green, long, narrow, basal blades, 8-20" (20-50 cm) long, partially folded down their centers, smooth wavy edges; a few smaller stem leaves

Fruit: tan pod, ½" (1 cm) long

Bloom: middle Feb-May, following rain

Cycle/Origin: perennial; native

Zone/Habitat: desert scrub below 2,500' (760 m); sand dunes, flats, rocky hills, mesas, among creosotebushes

Range: western third of Arizona

Notes: The sweetly fragrant flower looks similar to the cultivated Easter Lily. The only species in the genus, and recent studies have shown it may be more closely related to succulent yuccas and agaves. In spring, can be seen at the edges of sand dunes by the air-base near Yuma, Arizona. Also called Ajo Lily for the garlic-flavored bulbs, which were dug up and eaten by American Indians and early Spanish settlers (*ajo* is Spanish for "garlic"). The deeply buried bulbs can remain dormant for years, awaiting enough moisture to grow.

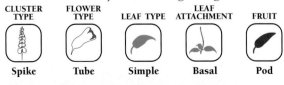

CLUSTER TYPE	FLOWER TYPE	LEAF TYPE	LEAF ATTACHMENT	FRUIT
Spike	Tube	Simple	Basal	Pod

FOOTHILL DEERVETCH
Lotus humistratus

Family: Pea or Bean (Fabaceae)

Height: 2-4" (5-10 cm)

Flower: tiny pea-like yellow flowers, ⅛" (.3 cm) long, turning red with age

Leaf: very hairy leaves, ½" (1 cm) long, are palmate, divided into 4 tiny oval leaflets with pointed tips

Fruit: erect oblong tan pod, ½" (1 cm) long

Bloom: Mar-Jun

Cycle/Origin: annual; native

Zone/Habitat: desert scrub, grasslands, oak/pinyon pine/juniper woodlands below 5,500' (1,675 m); rocky slopes, flats, along roads

Range: two-thirds of Arizona, in a wide band from the northwestern to southeastern corners of the state

Notes: A very common plant in deserts and grasslands. Foothill Deervetch forms dense, low-growing mats made up of hairy, succulent-looking small leaves and even tinier flowers. It is now more often being used in landscaping, as it makes a good ground cover. This nutritious member of the Pea and Bean family is very important to the desert tortoise–the leaves comprise a third of the tortoise's spring diet. Exotic non-native plants that crowd out native species are not eaten by desert tortoises and threaten their survival. The seeds are one of the main foods that Gambel's Quail and Scaled Quail eat year-round.

FLOWER TYPE	LEAF TYPE	LEAF ATTACHMENT	FRUIT
Irregular	Palmate	Alternate	Pod

MANY-BRISTLED CINCHWEED
Pectis papposa

Family: Aster (Asteraceae)

Height: 4-10" (10-25 cm)

Flower: small yellow flower head, ¼-½" (.6-1 cm) wide, is daisy-like and made up of 8 pointed petals (ray flowers) around a small yellow center; groups of blossoms loosely arranged at tops of sticky stems

Leaf: thread-like, dark green leaves, ½-2½" (1-6 cm) long, several pairs of bristles and sticky glands on the edges; oppositely attached to low branching stem

Bloom: Jul-Nov, but only after summer monsoons

Cycle/Origin: annual; native

Zone/Habitat: desert scrub below 5,000' (1,525 m); flats, along roads, sandy dunes, rocky slopes

Range: throughout Arizona, except the northeastern corner of the state

Notes: This plant forms low mounds covered with loose clusters of yellow composite blooms. Found in most of the Southwest, it flowers only after summer rains. In good years it can dominate the landscape, covering large expanses of desert. The only annual that blooms in the summer in the Mojave Desert, where rain rarely falls during that season. This flower is common in the Cabeza Prieta National Wildlife Refuge of southwestern Arizona, which has over 1,000 square miles (385 sq. km) of wilderness.

FLOWER TYPE

Composite

LEAF TYPE

Simple

LEAF ATTACHMENT

Opposite

fruit

SLENDER JANUSIA
Janusia gracilis

Family: Malpighia (Malpighiaceae)

Height: 6-9' (1.8-2.7 m); vine

Flower: lemon yellow flowers, ½" (1 cm) wide, have 5 wrinkled spoon-shaped petals around a green center

Leaf: narrowly lance-shaped leaves, ½-1½" (1-4 cm) long, are green, hairy above and below, and oppositely attached along slender twining grayish stems

Fruit: reddish seedpods, 1" (2.5 cm) wide, with 2-3 flat thin wings, fuzzy with white hairs

Bloom: Apr-Oct

Cycle/Origin: perennial; native

Zone/Habitat: desert scrub at 1,000-5,000' (305-1,525 m); along roads and washes, flats, rocky slopes

Range: southern half and northwestern corner of Arizona

Notes: Aptly named *gracilis* for its graceful appearance, this slender, twining, climbing vine grows on and entangled with cacti, desert trees and shrubs. The odd flowers with their paddle-shaped petals are soon followed by the fuzzy winged red seedpods. Vegetarian desert tortoises feed on the foliage and pods. This short-lived perennial grows only in small areas of southwestern New Mexico and Texas, although it is widespread in Arizona and northern Mexico. Slender Janusia can be easily found along the roadways in Saguaro National Park, located west of Tucson.

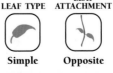

FLOWER TYPE	LEAF TYPE	LEAF ATTACHMENT	FRUIT
Regular	Simple	Opposite	Pod

WRIGHT DEERVETCH
Lotus wrightii

Family: Pea or Bean (Fabaceae)

Height: 8-16" (20-40 cm)

Flower: pea-like yellow flower, ½" (1 cm) long, turning orange or red; upper petal (standard) is rust colored below and flares backward

Leaf: dark green leaves, divided into 3-5 oblong narrow leaflets of differing sizes from ¼-½" (.6-1 cm) long; trailing, reclining stem; leaves turn red in autumn

Fruit: bean-like, greenish red pod, turning brown, ⅝-1" (1.5-2.5 cm) long, is slender and flattened

Bloom: Apr-Sep

Cycle/Origin: perennial; native

Zone/Habitat: oak/pinyon pine/juniper woods, riparian deciduous montane at 4,500-9,000' (1,370-2,745 m); among ponderosa pines, canyons, meadows

Range: throughout, except the southwestern corner

Notes: This upright or trailing, vine-like plant has conspicuous bright yellow blooms and is often found along streams in canyons. There are several stems arising from the base, but the stems have very few branches. Slow-growing and tolerant of dry or cold conditions. It sheds its leaves in the winter, dying back to the ground, and grows from the root in the spring. Fire-adapted, Wright Deervetch actually increases in abundance following high-intensity fires, which have been occurring more frequently in the Southwest.

FLOWER TYPE	LEAF TYPE	LEAF ATTACHMENT	FRUIT
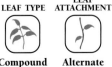			
Irregular	Compound	Alternate	Pod

MANY-FLOWERED PUCCOON
Lithospermum multiflorum

Family: Forget-me-not (Boraginaceae)

Height: 6-24" (15-61 cm)

Flower: groups of 2-10 trumpet-shaped, drooping yellow flowers; each flower, ½" (1 cm) wide, has a wide mouth with 5 rounded lobes; base of the flower is clasped by 5 slender pointed hairy bracts

Leaf: bluish green leaves, 1-2½" (2.5-6 cm) long, are long, thin and hairy with margins rolled under; upper leaves are gradually smaller; 2-3 small bracts at each leaf attachment (axis); hairy single stem

Bloom: Jun-Sep

Cycle/Origin: perennial; native

Zone/Habitat: pinyon pine/juniper woodlands, montane and sub-alpine at 6,000-9,500' (1,830-2,895 m); on slopes, along streams, limestone soils

Range: northern half and southeastern corner of Arizona

Notes: Often found under Ponderosa Pines, this hairy, erect plant has a single slender stem topped with a group of yellow tubular flowers. The genus name *Lithospermum* is from the words for "stone" and "seed," referring to the very hard, ripe nutlets that look like tiny polished stones. These stony nutlets were traditionally eaten by American Indians. The root was used for medicinal purposes and as a purple dye. In fact, "Puccoon" in the common name is an American Indian word referring to plants that yield dyes.

FLOWER TYPE	LEAF TYPE	LEAF ATTACHMENT
Tube	Simple	Alternate

DOGWEED
Thymophylla pentachaeta

Family: Aster (Asteraceae)

Height: 4-8" (10-20 cm)

Flower: small, daisy-like, yellow flower head, ½" (1 cm) wide, has 12-21 (usually 13) short oval petals around a wide, orangish yellow center of many tiny disk flowers; each bloom on its own, nearly leafless stalk well above the leaves

Leaf: stiffly lobed, sticky, slightly fuzzy leaves, 1" (2.5 cm) long, divided into 3-5 (usually 5) thread-like lobes with pointed prickly tips; leaves on lower half of the stem only; the plant has many densely leafy stems

Bloom: Mar-Sep

Cycle/Origin: perennial; native

Zone/Habitat: desert scrub at 2,500-4,500' (760-1,370 m); on flats, slopes, roadsides

Range: throughout Arizona, except the southwestern and northeastern corners of the state

Notes: A very common, low-growing perennial found on desert flats. Often seen growing along roadways and in natural areas of Tucson. The individual small flower heads are inconspicuous, but a yellow haze appears to float above the desert floor after heavy rains, when mats of Dogweed bloom. The aromatic leaves are required food for the caterpillars of the tiny Dainty Sulphur butterfly. Also called Five-needle Pricklyleaf for the needle-like lobes of the leaves.

FLOWER TYPE — **Composite**

LEAF TYPE — **Simple Lobed**

LEAF ATTACHMENT — **Opposite**

297

SWEETBUSH
Bebbia juncea

Family: Aster (Asteraceae)

Height: 1-4' (30-122 cm); shrub

Flower: button-like, yellow flower head, ½" (1 cm) wide, is rayless, made up of tiny disk flowers only and clasped by fuzzy, pointed, whitish green bracts with tips that curl downward; leafless fuzzy flower stalk

Leaf: few lance-shaped leaves, ½-1" (1-2.5 cm) long, have smooth edges (sometimes lobed) with pointed tips, are rough and hairy, oppositely attached to hairy stems; leaves fall off during drought

Bloom: Apr-Jul

Cycle/Origin: perennial; native

Zone/Habitat: desert scrub below 4,000' (1,220 m); rocky slopes, among creosotebushes, flats, plateaus, along washes

Range: throughout Arizona, except the northeastern corner

Notes: This densely branched shrub forms a naturally rounded bush that is leafless most of the year. The thin green stems continue to make food (photosynthesis) during dry periods when the leaves have all dropped off. The stems have fuzzy white hairs that decrease the evaporation of water from the pores in their surface. The yellow blooms of this perennial are never numerous enough to obscure the green branches, but they do attract butterflies to their nectar. Also called Chuckwalla's Delight, as the plant is a favorite food of the Chuckwalla, a large native vegetarian lizard.

FLOWER TYPE	LEAF TYPE	LEAF ATTACHMENT
	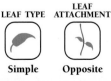	
Composite	Simple	Opposite

AMERICAN THREEFOLD
Trixis californica

Family: Aster (Asteraceae)

Height: 12-36" (30-91 cm); shrub

Flower: yellow flower head, ½-¾" (1-2 cm) wide, that appears to have petals (ray flowers), but actually has 9-15 tubular disk flowers flaring out into two yellow lips; lower lip is petal-like and upper lip is tightly coiled backward; conspicuous male flowers parts (anthers) protrude well above each disk flower

Leaf: narrowly lance-shaped, yellowish green leaves, 1-2" (2.5-5 cm) long, are evergreen, rigid, have margins rolled under and winged leafstalks; leafy stiff stems

Bloom: Feb-Oct, mostly in spring, but anytime after rain

Cycle/Origin: perennial; native

Zone/Habitat: desert scrub, grasslands, oak/pinyon pine woodlands below 5,500' (1,675 m); gravel slopes, flats

Range: throughout Arizona, except the northeastern corner

Notes: The unique fragrant flower heads appear to have ray flowers around the center like other asters, but the petals are actually the extended outer lip of the tubular disk flowers. The many dense, foul-smelling leaves get progressively smaller up the stem to just under the blooms. Also called Plumilla, Spanish for "little feather," for the tufts of golden bristles on its seed-like fruit. The Seri Indians, who live along the Gulf of California, believe this plant has important medicinal properties.

FLOWER TYPE	LEAF TYPE	LEAF ATTACHMENT	LEAF ATTACHMENT

Composite	Simple	Alternate	Whorl

GREENLEAF FIVE EYES
Chamaesaracha coronopus

Family: Nightshade (Solanaceae)

Height: 6-18" (15-45 cm)

Flower: pale greenish yellow-to-cream, star-shaped flower, ⅓-¾" (.8-2 cm) wide, of fused fuzzy sepals and petals held by globe-shaped green calyx; each petal has a raised yellow or white spot at the base

Leaf: narrowly lance-shaped leaves, 1-4" (2.5-10 cm) long, are thick and rough, hairy with wavy margins

Fruit: berry-like yellowish fruit, ¼" (.6 cm) wide, has dark brown seeds; persistent 5-lobed papery calyx

Bloom: Apr-Sep

Cycle/Origin: perennial; native

Zone/Habitat: desert scrub, grasslands, interior chaparral, pinyon pine/juniper woods at 2,500-7,500' (760-2,285 m); abandoned fields, mesas, plains

Range: scattered locations throughout Arizona, but mostly in the northern and central parts of the state

Notes: This low-growing plant is also called Small Groundcherry or Prostrate Groundcherry for its yellow fruit and sprawling stems. The mounded yellow or white spot at the base of each narrow petal gives rise to "Five Eyes" in the common name. Different from the closely related Velvet Hairy Five Eyes (*C. sordida*) (not shown), which lacks spots on its petals and is found only near water.

FLOWER TYPE

Regular

LEAF TYPE

Simple

LEAF ATTACHMENT

Alternate

FRUIT

Berry

fruit

GORDON BLADDERPOD
Lesquerella gordonii

Family: Mustard (Brassicaceae)

Height: 4-16" (10-40 cm)

Flower: loose groups of bright yellow flowers; each flower, ¾" (2 cm) wide, has 4 oval petals that are shallowly notched at the tips

Leaf: oblong or lance-shaped, grayish green basal leaves, ½-3" (1-7.5 cm) long, variable margins; stem leaves are smaller, narrower; stems often lie on the ground

Fruit: nearly spherical, smooth green pod, ⅜" (.9 cm) wide, with a lengthwise brown band and tipped with thread-like projection; turns brown with age

Bloom: Feb-May

Cycle/Origin: annual, perennial, biennial; native

Zone/Habitat: desert scrub at 100-5,000' (30-1,525 m); on flats, along washes, slopes, under shrubs

Range: southernmost quarter of Arizona

Notes: In Arizona, this showy mustard is limited to only four counties in the south. After good winter rains it occurs in huge patches on flats among creosotebushes. Especially obvious and abundant in northeastern Tucson along the popular Catalina Highway, which goes up Mount Lemmon in the Santa Catalina Mountains. When stepped on, the seedpods make a popping sound, hence another common name, Popweed. Ranges east to Texas and north to Kansas.

FLOWER TYPE	LEAF TYPE	LEAF TYPE	LEAF ATTACHMENT	LEAF ATTACHMENT	FRUIT
Regular	Simple	Simple Lobed	Alternate	Basal	Pod

CALIFORNIA SUNCUP
Camissonia californica

Family: Evening-primrose (Onagraceae)

Height: 2-4' (61-122 cm)

Flower: yellow flowers, ¾" (2 cm) wide, have 4 oval petals with red spots at the bases and protruding yellow flower parts

Leaf: narrowly elliptical, dark green basal leaves, 2-6" (5-15 cm) long, have irregular pairs of sharp-pointed lobes; smaller stem leaves are sparse, narrower and smooth edged or toothed

Fruit: orangish red seedpod, 2-4" (5-10 cm) long, is long and slender, 4-angled and bends downward

Bloom: Feb-Jun

Cycle/Origin: annual, perennial; native

Zone/Habitat: desert scrub, grasslands, interior chaparral below 5,000' (1,525 m); along washes, slopes, roadsides

Range: western half of Arizona

Notes: This spindly wildflower has multi-branched, smooth, erect, dark green stems that bear a few scattered, bright yellow flowers. The flowers open in the evening and close by the following midday. Although a member of the Evening-primrose family, it resembles a mustard and is sometimes called Mustard Evening-primrose. This plant is so well adapted to wildfires in chaparral life zones that the seeds germinate best when first exposed to smoke.

FLOWER TYPE	LEAF TYPE	LEAF TYPE	LEAF ATTACHMENT	LEAF ATTACHMENT	FRUIT
Regular	Simple	Simple Lobed	Alternate	Basal	Pod

fruit

HOARY INDIAN MALLOW
Abutilon incanum

Family: Mallow (Malvaceae)

Height: 3-6' (.9-1.8 m)

Flower: orangish yellow or white flowers, ¾" (2 cm) wide, have 5 broad petals around a yellow and red center

Leaf: elongated heart-shaped, velvety, grayish green leaves, ½-3" (1-7.5 cm) long, with scalloped or toothed edges and pointed tips; upper leaves much smaller or absent

Fruit: bowl-shaped dry yellow capsule, ½" (1 cm) wide, splits into 5 segments

Bloom: Mar-Oct

Cycle/Origin: perennial; native

Zone/Habitat: desert scrub at 1,000-4,500' (305-1,370 m); rocky flats, dry slopes, arroyos, along roads

Range: southern half and northwestern quarter of Arizona

Notes: This perennial is found in the Sonoran Desert in Arizona, but not in the Mojave Desert. The upright stems branch near the base and are less leafy higher up the stems. Like all plants in the Mallow family, the numerous male flowers parts (stamens) are fused to form a central column, and the petals of the buds are twisted. The flowers of Hoary Indian Mallow can also be pink or white with round petals around a red center. Also called Sweet Pelotazo.

FLOWER TYPE	LEAF TYPE	LEAF ATTACHMENT	FRUIT
Regular	Simple	Alternate	Pod

SHRUBBY DEERVETCH
Lotus rigidus

Family: Pea or Bean (Fabaceae)

Height: 6-36" (15-91 cm)

Flower: pea-like yellow (sometimes orange-tinged) flower, ¾" (2 cm) long, upper petal (standard) flares backward and is rust-colored on the back; flower is clasped by hairy, reddish green sepals (calyx); unopened buds are reddish orange

Leaf: leaves are alternate and widely spaced along several erect wiry stems; each leaf, ½-1" (1-2.5 cm) long, is divided into 3-4 oblong leaflets of uneven sizes

Fruit: narrow, straight, oblong smooth seedpod, ¾-1½" (2-4 cm) long, is green, turning reddish brown

Bloom: Feb-May

Cycle/Origin: perennial; native

Zone/Habitat: desert scrub, interior chaparral, pinyon pine/juniper woodlands at 200-5,500' (60-1,675 m); flats

Range: throughout Arizona, except the southeastern corner

Notes: This upright, broom-like, wild pea frequently grows in soil that collects in boulder crevices. The species name *rigidus* and another common name, Wiry Lotus, describe the stiff wire-like stems that branch several times. With fewer leaves than other species of *Lotus* in Arizona, it is better adapted to dry conditions, often blooming even during drought.

FLOWER TYPE	LEAF TYPE	LEAF ATTACHMENT	FRUIT
Irregular	Palmate	Alternate	Pod

BUTTON BRITTLEBUSH
Encelia frutescens

Family: Aster (Asteraceae)

Height: 2-4' (61-122 cm); shrub

Flower: yellow-orange flower head, ¾" (2 cm) wide, is button-shaped, usually lacks petals (ray flowers) and has only tiny tubular yellow disk flowers; has protruding orange flower parts and white-haired green bracts; flower heads at tips of hairy stems

Leaf: oval, shiny, dark green leaves, ½-1" (1-2.5 cm) long, have stiff hairs below and on wavy edges

Bloom: Feb-May and Aug-Sep, after rainfall

Cycle/Origin: perennial; native

Zone/Habitat: desert scrub below 4,000' (1,220 m); rocky slopes, mesas, flats, arroyos, roadsides

Range: throughout Arizona, except the southeastern corner

Notes: This plant is sometimes called Green Brittlebush for the color of the leaves, which can be distinguished from the bluish green leaves of Brittlebush (pg. 357). Aptly named *frutescens*, which means "shrubby" in Latin, this multi-branched perennial has pinkish stems that turn whitish as they age. The solitary, disk-shaped flower heads tipping the stems have disk flowers and usually lack ray flowers, thus it is also called Rayless Encelia.

FLOWER TYPE	LEAF TYPE	LEAF ATTACHMENT
Composite	**Simple**	**Alternate**

CAMPHORWEED
Heterotheca subaxillaris

Family: Aster (Asteraceae)

Height: 1-5' (30-152 cm)

Flower: daisy-like yellow flower head, ½-1" (1-2.5 cm) wide, composed of 15-30 petals (ray flowers) and a yellow-orange center (disk flowers); many flower heads per plant atop the branched upper stem

Leaf: oval leaves, 1-4" (2.5-10 cm) long, have smooth or slightly toothed margins, are stalked and alternate lower on the stem; leaves along middle and upper stem are stalkless and clasping; leaves and the single stem are hairy and sticky due to glands in the hairs

Bloom: Mar-Nov

Cycle/Origin: annual, biennial; native

Zone/Habitat: desert scrub and grasslands at 1,000-5,500' (305-1,525 m); along roads, disturbed sites, open areas, old fields, dunes

Range: central and southeastern Arizona

Notes: This sparsely or densely leaved aster is named for the camphor-like odor emitted from its leaves when crushed. It is very weedy and drought tolerant. Ranchers dislike it because cows avoid eating it, and the plant can overtake pastures. However, it does serve as food for the caterpillars of several moth species. When applied to injuries, such as sprains or bruises, the foliage is said to diminish pain, inflammation and swelling.

FLOWER TYPE	LEAF TYPE	LEAF ATTACHMENT	LEAF ATTACHMENT

Composite	Simple	Alternate	Clasping

SEEP MONKEYFLOWER
Mimulus guttatus

Family: Snapdragon (Scrophulariaceae)

Height: 2-36" (5-91 cm)

Flower: loose groups of vivid yellow flowers; each tubular flower, ⅜-1½" (.9-4 cm) long, has erect upper 2-lobed petal (lip) and 3-lobed lower lip; swollen, hairy, red-spotted patches nearly close the throat

Leaf: fleshy, dark green leaves, ½-4" (1-10 cm) long, are round and coarsely toothed; upper leaves are much smaller and stalkless; fleshy-walled stems are hollow

Fruit: oval brown pod, ½" (1 cm) long, thickest in the middle, tapering at both ends

Bloom: Mar-Sep

Cycle/Origin: annual, perennial; native

Zone/Habitat: riparian deciduous in all life zones at 500-9,500' (150-2,895 m); seeps, along washes, streambeds

Range: throughout

Notes: This plant can be tall and spindly, or short and bushy. Mostly found on land at seeps, along streams or near springs, but sometimes found floating in water with its roots submerged. Will take advantage of the smallest bit of moist sand to grow at the bottom of a desert wash, surprising hikers with its vivid flowers. American Indians ate the succulent leaves as salad greens. *Guttatus* means "specks," referring to the red spots on the lower petals.

FLOWER TYPE	LEAF TYPE	LEAF ATTACHMENT	FRUIT
Irregular	Simple	Opposite	Pod

SPREADING FANPETALS
Sida abutifolia

Family: Mallow (Malvaceae)

Height: 12-24" (30-61 cm); vine

Flower: dull brownish yellow flower, 1" (2.5 cm) wide, has 5 broad fan-shaped petals with notched edges and yellow-to-green bases, surrounding bright yellow flower parts; backed by shorter, light green sepals fused into the shape of a star

Leaf: hairy, dark green leaves, ½-1" (1-2.5 cm) long, narrowly lance-shaped, folded lengthwise, scalloped reddish margins; reddish hairy sprawling stems

Fruit: triangular capsule, ¼" (.6 cm) wide, is yellowish to tan and contains many tiny seeds

Bloom: Apr-Oct

Cycle/Origin: annual, perennial; non-native

Zone/Habitat: desert scrub and grasslands at 2,500-6,000' (760-1,830 m); open areas, plateaus, flats, along roads

Range: southern half of Arizona, except the southwestern edge of the state

Notes: The branched hairs covering the leaves and stems are typical of plants in the Mallow family, as are the fused male flower parts (stamens) forming a column in the center. This low-growing herb that prefers disturbed areas has become a troublesome invasive weed in some situations such as in irrigated fields. Introduced to Arizona, but now naturalized in about half of the state.

FLOWER TYPE	LEAF TYPE	LEAF ATTACHMENT	FRUIT
Regular	Simple	Alternate	Pod

WHITESTEM PAPERFLOWER
Psilostrophe cooperi

Family: Aster (Asteraceae)

Height: 6-24" (15-61 cm); shrub

Flower: bright yellow flower head, 1" (2.5 cm) wide, with 3-6 non-overlapping broad petals; each petal is tipped with 3 shallow lobes, folded at its base and appears inserted into the small yellow center

Leaf: narrowly lance-shaped, grayish green leaves, ½-3½" (1-9 cm) long, have whitish hairs, pointed tips and alternate along whitish stems; upper leaves smaller

Bloom: mostly Apr-Jun, but sometimes year-round

Cycle/Origin: perennial; native

Zone/Habitat: desert scrub, grasslands, oak/pinyon pine/juniper woods at 300-8,300' (90-2,530 m); along washes, among creosotebushes, plateaus, slopes

Range: throughout Arizona, except the northeastern and southwestern corners of the state

Notes: Whitestem Paperflower is an open, branching shrub with matted woolly white hairs covering the stems. It forms a tangled, grayish green mound that is covered with brilliant yellow when its flowers bloom. This common roadside wildflower is sometimes called Paper Daisy because the dried blooms, which remain on the plant for several weeks, look like daisies made of translucent tan paper. The dried flowers have been used in floral arrangements.

FLOWER TYPE	LEAF TYPE	LEAF ATTACHMENT
Composite	**Simple**	**Alternate**

LACY TANSY-ASTER
Machaeranthera pinnatifida

Family: Aster (Asteraceae)

Height: 8-24" (20-61 cm)

Flower: daisy-like, golden yellow flower head, 1" (2.5 cm) wide, with layers of 30-45 narrow overlapping (can be non-overlapping) petals around an orangish yellow center; clasped below by layers of pointed, bristle-tipped, erect bracts

Leaf: oblong to spoon-shaped, grayish green leaves, ½-2½" (1-6 cm) long, are stalkless and have pairs of narrow lobes with smooth or toothed margins that are always tipped with bristly hairs; upper leaves tiny; thin woolly stems; branches are interwoven

Bloom: Feb-May

Cycle/Origin: perennial; native

Zone/Habitat: desert scrub, grasslands, oak/pinyon pine/juniper woodlands at 2,100-5,000' (640-1,525 m); in open areas

Range: throughout

Notes: Lacy Tansy-aster leaves and flowers are highly variable. Look for the solitary, golden yellow flowers that appear to float above the erect branches, since the leaves are tiny on the upper stems. "Lacy" in the common name is for the feather-like leaves found on the lower half of the stems. Also called Cutleaf Iron Plant for the lobed leaves and its woody base, which is very hard when dried.

FLOWER TYPE
Composite

LEAF TYPE
Simple

LEAF TYPE
Simple Lobed

LEAF ATTACHMENT
Alternate

leaves

FINELEAF HYMENOPAPPUS
Hymenopappus filifolius

Family: Aster (Asteraceae)

Height: 12-30" (30-76 cm)

Flower: golden yellow flower heads, 1" (2.5 cm) wide, are round and spiky, on long thin leafless stalks; each blossom is made up of enlarged disk flowers only (no ray flowers) with protruding flower parts and is cupped by fuzzy whitish green bracts

Leaf: grayish green, woolly basal leaves, 3-8" (7.5-20 cm) long, are sticky, usually feather-like and divided into thread-like lobes; can be simple and narrowly oval; sometimes a few much smaller leaves along stem

Bloom: May-Sep

Cycle/Origin: perennial; native

Zone/Habitat: interior chaparral, oak/pinyon pine/juniper woodlands, montane at 3,500-7,500' (1,065-2,285 m); scattered among pines, dry rocky slopes, mesas

Range: throughout, except the southwestern corner

Notes: In Arizona, this widespread aster has slim leafless stalks topped by a few solitary blooms and is easily overlooked. *Filifolius* means "thread-like leaf," referring to the thin lobes of the feathery leaves that form low round clumps of foliage (see inset). It is found in every state west of the Mississippi River. A similar species, the Mexican Woollywhite (*H. mexicanus*) (not shown), is found higher in the mountains at elevations up to 10,000 feet (3,050 m).

FLOWER TYPE	LEAF TYPE	LEAF TYPE	LEAF ATTACHMENT	LEAF ATTACHMENT
Composite	**Simple**	**Simple Lobed**	**Alternate**	**Basal**

UPRIGHT PRAIRIE CONEFLOWER
Ratibida columnifera

Family: Aster (Asteraceae)

Height: 12-36" (30-91 cm)

Flower: cylindrical yellowish brown cone, 1" (2.5 cm) tall, of hundreds of tiny disk flowers surrounded by 4-12 drooping oval petals (ray flowers) that are yellow, red or bicolored; 1-15 flower heads per plant, each on a long stalk above the leaves

Leaf: stiff thin leaves, ¾-6" (2-15 cm) long, have 3-14 long narrow uneven lobes, are hairy and alternately attached

Bloom: Jun-Nov

Cycle/Origin: perennial; native

Zone/Habitat: all life zones except subalpine at 800-7,500' (245-2,285 m); open areas in pine forests, along roads, grassy areas, disturbed ground

Range: northeastern third of Arizona

Notes: In the wild, this drought-tolerant prairie plant is widespread in the Great Plains of the Midwest, but it is also native to Arizona. Has been used in prairie restorations. A cultivated ornamental often grown in wildflower gardens, it frequently escapes to roadsides and prairie-like habitats. Cheyenne Indians made a solution from the leaves and stems that was applied to the skin to draw out poison from rattlesnake bites and for relief from Poison Ivy. Frequently called Mexican Hat, for the sombrero-like shape of the flower head.

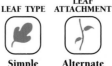

FLOWER TYPE	LEAF TYPE	LEAF ATTACHMENT
Composite	Simple Lobed	Alternate

SPINY SOW-THISTLE
Sonchus asper

Family: Aster (Asteraceae)

Height: 1-6' (.3-1.8 m)

Flower: dandelion-like yellow flower head, 1" (2.5 cm) wide, made up of slender petals (ray flowers) with fringed tips; many flower heads per plant

Leaf: lance- or spoon-shaped, shiny leaves, 2½-6" (6-15 cm) long, are dark green and stiff, with very wavy spiny margins and curled rounded bases that clasp the stems; upper leaves much smaller; branching, purplish green stem contains milky sap

Bloom: Feb-Nov

Cycle/Origin: annual; non-native

Zone/Habitat: most life zones at 150-7,000' (46-2,135 m), agricultural areas at lower elevations; disturbed sites, along railroads, roadsides, old fields

Range: throughout

Notes: Spiny Sow-thistle is an introduced plant that has become a very invasive weed, spreading over much of the United States. Like a dandelion, its seeds are dispersed by the wind. Due to its deep taproot and spiny leaves, this stout plant is hard to eradicate. A look-alike, Common Sow-thistle (*S. oleraceus*) (not shown), has leaves that are less spiny than Spiny Sow-thistle and a curled leaf base that tapers to a point at the outside of the curl, unlike the ear-shaped leaf base of this plant.

FLOWER TYPE	LEAF TYPE	LEAF TYPE	LEAF ATTACHMENT	LEAF ATTACHMENT
Composite	Simple	Simple Lobed	Alternate	Clasping

329

fruit

COVES CASSIA
Senna covesii

Family: Pea or Bean (Fabaceae)

Height: 12-24" (30-61 cm)

Flower: orangish yellow flower, ¾-1½" (2-4 cm) wide, has 4 oblong, non-overlapping petals around a few dark flower parts; groups of 3-9 flowers, at end of a stalk from a leaf junction (axis), bloom a few at a time

Leaf: dark bluish green leaves, 2" (5 cm) long, divided into 2-3 pairs of elliptical short-stalked leaflets, ½-1" (1-2.5 cm) long; leafy stems have dense white hairs

Fruit: slightly curved, oblong green pod, ¾-2" (2-5 cm) long, turns woody

Bloom: Apr-Oct, especially after warm rains

Cycle/Origin: perennial; native

Zone/Habitat: desert scrub at 1,000-3,000' (305-915 m); slopes

Range: throughout, except the northwestern corner

Notes: Also called Desert Senna for its habitat or Rattlebox for the dry rattling sound the woody seedpods make when shaken. Bumblebees and carpenter bees pollinate the flowers by a process called "buzz pollination." A bee lands on the flower and vibrates its flying muscles, causing the pollen to flow out of the anthers. The bee collects the pollen to eat later and inadvertently pollinates the next flower upon landing. An important food source for the caterpillars of Sleepy Orange and Cloudless Sulphur butterflies. The Seri Indians of Mexico used the root medicinally.

FLOWER TYPE	LEAF TYPE	LEAF ATTACHMENT	FRUIT
Regular	Compound	Alternate	Pod

GHOSTFLOWER
Mohavea confertiflora

Family: Snapdragon (Scrophulariaceae)

Height: 4-16" (10-40 cm)

Flower: deeply cup-shaped, translucent yellowish or cream flowers, 1-1½" (2.5-4 cm) long, are dotted with maroon inside; fused petals form a wide upper lip and a swollen base with large maroon spot; 2 bright yellow male flower parts (stamens)

Leaf: lance-shaped or long and thin, fuzzy leaves, ½-4" (1-10 cm) long, with pointed tips; upper leaves stick out between flowers at top of stem

Fruit: fragile tan pod, ½" (1 cm) long, is oval and opens through top pores, spilling winged seeds

Bloom: Feb-Apr

Cycle/Origin: annual; native

Zone/Habitat: desert scrub below 3,500' (1,065 m); gravelly flats, lower mountain slopes (bajadas), along washes

Range: northwestern and southwestern corners of Arizona

Notes: This true desert annual grows a short, unbranched stem when winter rains are few and a taller, branched stem when rainfall is plentiful. Has one to many blooms (also depending on the amount of moisture the plant receives) at leaf attachments. "Ghost" is for the translucent look of its blossoms and *confertiflora* means "crowded flowers." Found only in the lower deserts of western Arizona, southeastern California, Nevada and northern Mexico.

FLOWER TYPE	LEAF TYPE	LEAF ATTACHMENT	FRUIT
Irregular	Simple	Alternate	Pod

PLAINS ZINNIA
Zinnia grandiflora

Family: Aster (Asteraceae)

Height: 4-12" (10-30 cm); shrub

Flower: bright yellow flower heads, 1-1½" (2.5-4 cm) wide, have 3-6 round shallowly notched petals (ray flowers) around a reddish orange center (disk flowers)

Leaf: narrow leaves, 1-2" (2.5-5 cm) long, are light green, fuzzy and twisted; densely and oppositely attached along branching stems

Bloom: May-Oct

Cycle/Origin: perennial; native

Zone/Habitat: desert scrub, grasslands, oak/pinyon pine/juniper woodlands at 4,000-6,500' (1,220-1,980 m); along roads, hillsides, mesas, among grasses, dry soils

Range: northern half and southeastern corner of Arizona

Notes: A perennial shrub forming rounded mounds of foliage nearly completely covered with long-lasting yellow flowers. The flowers persist on the plant into fall, drying and turning papery and brown. Plains Zinnia spreads by underground stems (rhizomes) to form large colonies. Also called Rocky Mountain Zinnia, this Aster family member ranges from Arizona east to Texas and northeast to Kansas. Often cultivated as a ground cover and used in borders, as it is drought tolerant and cold hardy.

FLOWER TYPE

Composite

LEAF TYPE

Simple

LEAF ATTACHMENT

Opposite

CURLYCUP GUMWEED
Grindelia squarrosa

Family: Aster (Asteraceae)

Height: 12-36" (30-91 cm)

Flower: yellow, daisy-like flower head, 1-1½" (2.5-4 cm) wide, is atop layers of downward-curving green bracts; each bloom has 25-40 short oval overlapping petals around a darker yellow center

Leaf: variable-shaped leaves, from oval to spoon-shaped, 1-3" (2.5-7.5 cm) long, have coarse-toothed edges and are dotted with glands; middle and top leaves alternately clasp the multi-branched reddish stem

Bloom: Jul-Sep

Cycle/Origin: annual, perennial, biennial; non-native

Zone/Habitat: grasslands, interior chaparral, woodlands of oak/pinyon pine/juniper, montane at 4,000-7,500' (1,220-2,285 m); dry open areas, overgrazed land

Range: northern half of Arizona

Notes: Although this aster is extremely common along roads in northern Arizona, it was probably introduced to Arizona from the Great Plains, where it is thought to have originated. A tea made from the leaves and flowers was used by Plains Indian tribes to treat bronchitis. The species name *squarrosa* and "Curlycup" in the common name both refer to the conspicuous outward-curving bracts, which make this aster unusually easy to identify. The bracts have glands that exude a sticky resin, thus the name "Gumweed."

FLOWER TYPE	LEAF TYPE	LEAF ATTACHMENT	LEAF ATTACHMENT
Composite	Simple	Alternate	Clasping

THREADLEAF RAGWORT
Senecio flaccidus

Family: Aster (Asteraceae)

Height: 1-4' (30-122 cm); shrub

Flower: daisy-like flower, 1-1½" (2.5-4 cm) wide, of non-overlapping, narrow yellow petals (usually 8-17) surrounding an orangish center of disk flowers

Leaf: thread-like, bluish green leaves, 1½-4" (4-10 cm) long, divided into very narrow lobes, smooth or woolly and covered with matted gray hairs; leaves are alternately attached to the stiff stem

Bloom: May-Nov, but year-round in low elevations

Cycle/Origin: perennial; native

Zone/Habitat: desert scrub, grasslands and interior chaparral at 2,500-7,500' (760-2,285 m); along sandy washes, disturbed or overgrazed lands, flats, plateaus

Range: throughout

Notes: This many stemmed, multi-branched, bluish green shrub has bright yellow flowers on long stalks at the end of the branches. Abundant in disturbed soils or overgrazed lands, it stabilizes the soil, which helps other plants to become established. Toxic if eaten by livestock, but American Indians once used this plant medicinally. Navajo Indians boiled the plant and drank the liquid to aid their voices in ceremonial singing and used the flower heads to brush spines off of cactus fruit.

FLOWER TYPE	LEAF TYPE	LEAF ATTACHMENT
Composite	Simple Lobed	Alternate

white form

CALIFORNIA POPPY
Eschscholzia californica

Family: Poppy (Papaveraceae)

Height: 2-16" (5-40 cm)

Flower: shallowly cup-shaped, yellow or orangish yellow flower, 1½" (4 cm) wide, has 4 fan-shaped petals, each with an orange spot at the base; each flower on a single stalk; many flowers per plant

Leaf: fern-like, bluish green basal leaves, 2½" (6 cm) long, with 3 thin rounded lobes; few stem leaves

Fruit: erect, cylindrical, pointed green pod, 4" (10 cm) long, splits open to release tiny black seeds

Bloom: middle Feb-May

Cycle/Origin: annual; native

Zone/Habitat: desert scrub below 4,600' (1,400 m); flats, slopes

Range: throughout, except the northeastern part of the state

Notes: The blooms of California Poppy remain open only in full sunlight, closing at night and when cloudy. After heavy winter rains, acres of desert floor are densely carpeted with the gold flowers of California Poppy mixed with Arroyo Lupine (pg. 43) and Fiddleneck (pg. 415). Blooms can be pinkish white or white (see inset). Sometimes hikers find the flowers on stalks that are thigh-high. The small annual poppies in Arizona were long considered to be a separate species called Mexican Poppy (*E. mexicana*), but they are now thought to be a subspecies of California Poppy.

FLOWER TYPE	LEAF TYPE	LEAF ATTACHMENT	LEAF ATTACHMENT	FRUIT
Regular	Simple Lobed	Alternate	Basal	Pod

seed head

PALE AGOSERIS
Agoseris glauca

Family: Aster (Asteraceae)

Height: 1-10" (2.5-25 cm)

Flower: dandelion-like yellow flower head, 1½" (4 cm) wide, has layers of numerous yellow petals (ray flowers) with dark lines below and notched tips, around a few yellow flower parts; held by a hairy triangular purple-spotted green bract; flower tops a single leafless hairy stem

Leaf: narrow, grass-like or lance-shaped basal leaves, 6-14" (15-36 cm) long, are purplish blue-green or with a purplish central vein

Bloom: May-Oct

Cycle/Origin: perennial; native

Zone/Habitat: higher desert scrub, montane, subalpine at 6,500-10,000' (1,980-3,050 m); among coniferous trees, along roads, in sagebrush scrub

Range: northern half of Arizona, scattered in the south central part of the state

Notes: Also called Mountain Dandelion for the flower heads and resulting fluffy globe-like seed heads (see inset), which look very much like the smaller puffballs of Common Dandelion (pg. 345). The hairy leafless stems contain a milky sap. First collected by Lewis and Clark on their famous expedition to the American West. *Glauca* means "blue-green" in Latin, referring to the color of the leaves.

FLOWER TYPE	LEAF TYPE	LEAF ATTACHMENT
		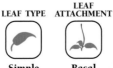
Composite	Simple	Basal

COMMON DANDELION
Taraxacum officinale

Family: Aster (Asteraceae)

Height: 2-18" (5-45 cm)

Flower: appears to be 1 large yellow flower, 1½" (4 cm) wide, but is actually a composite of many tiny flowers that are clustered together

Leaf: a rosette of dark green basal leaves, 2-8" (5-20 cm) long, with deep lobes and sharp teeth

Bloom: year-round

Cycle/Origin: perennial; non-native

Zone/Habitat: all life zones below 9,000' (2,745 m); disturbed sites, lawns, roadsides, along trails

Range: eastern two-thirds of Arizona

Notes: This non-native perennial is responsible for much water contamination, as people treat lawns with chemicals to eradicate Common Dandelion. In French, *dent-de-lion* refers to the toothed leaves, which resemble the teeth of a lion. Its flowers open in mornings and close in afternoons. The globe-like seed heads have soft hair-like bristles that resemble tiny parachutes, which carry the seeds away on the wind. Originally brought from Eurasia as a food crop. Its leaves are bitter, but offer high vitamin and mineral content. The long taproot has been roasted and ground to use as a coffee substitute.

FLOWER
TYPE

Composite

LEAF TYPE

Simple
Lobed

LEAF
ATTACHMENT

Basal

ANGELITA DAISY
Tetraneuris acaulis

Family: Aster (Asteraceae)

Height: 3-12" (7.5-30 cm)

Flower: daisy-like flower head, 1-2" (2.5-5 cm) wide, has 8-15 long, narrow, non-overlapping yellow petals that have dark lines on the undersides, 3-lobed tips and surround a yellow center

Leaf: narrowly lance-shaped basal leaves, ¾-2½" (2-6 cm) long, with pointed tips and densely dotted with glands that make them sticky

Bloom: Apr-Oct

Cycle/Origin: perennial; native

Zone/Habitat: pinyon pine/juniper woodlands and montane at 4,000-6,000' (1,220-1,830 m); among ponderosa pines, plateaus, rocky slopes

Range: northern half of Arizona, often planted in gardens in Phoenix

Notes: Also known as Arizona Four-nerve Daisy, this cheery yellow flower is often grown in gardens at low elevations. It is especially popular among Phoenix gardeners since it is drought tolerant and hardy in temperatures as low as 10°F (-12°C). Even in desert locations, this plant blooms most of the summer if watered weekly. The yellow blooms top leafless, slightly fuzzy flower stalks well above the basal rosette of leaves, but this plant has no leafy stems. In fact, the species name *acaulis* is Greek, meaning "without stems."

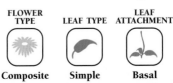

FLOWER TYPE	LEAF TYPE	LEAF ATTACHMENT
Composite	Simple	Basal

ARIZONA YELLOWBELLS
Tecoma stans

Family: Trumpet Creeper (Bignoniaceae)

Height: 2-15' (.6-4.6 m); shrub

Flower: groups of 2-7 trumpet-shaped, golden flowers, 1-2" (2.5-5 cm) long, with orange-striped throats; each flower has 5 fused petals that flare into rounded notched lobes and a short crown-like green calyx

Leaf: shiny, dark green leaves, 6" (15 cm) long, divided into 5-13 narrowly oval leaflets, 2-5" (5-13 cm) long, with pointed tips and sharp-toothed edges

Fruit: long, thin, dangling tan pod, 3-8" (7.5-20 cm) long

Bloom: May-Oct

Cycle/Origin: perennial; native

Zone/Habitat: desert scrub, grasslands, oak/juniper woodlands at 3,000-5,500' (915-1,675 m); rocky slopes, canyons

Range: southeastern quarter of Arizona, often cultivated throughout the state

Notes: Found in only four states in the wild in the U.S. Occurs naturally and abundantly along Box Canyon Road in the Santa Rita Mountains, located south of Tucson. This stunning bush is evergreen in frost-free areas, attaining woody stems and its maximum, tree-like height. When frozen back to the ground in temperatures near 20°F (-7°C), it recovers readily and sends out new green shoots the next spring, but doesn't grow more than 3 feet (.9 m) tall.

FLOWER TYPE

Tube

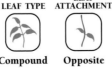

LEAF TYPE

Compound

LEAF ATTACHMENT

Opposite

FRUIT

Pod

HARTWEG SUNDROPS
Calylophus hartwegii

Family: Evening-primrose (Onagraceae)

Height: 12-16" (30-40 cm)

Flower: large yellow (fading to pinkish) flower, 1-2½" (2.5-6 cm) wide, made up of 4 wide (almost square) wrinkled petals; center is same color as the petals

Leaf: narrowly oval, grayish green basal leaves, ½-1½" (1-4 cm) long, have fuzzy stem leaves; sometimes clusters of smaller leaves grow in leaf attachments

Fruit: 4-parted, cylindrical green pod, ¼-1½" (.6-4 cm) long, fuzzy with white hairs, has many tiny seeds

Bloom: Apr-Jun

Cycle/Origin: perennial; native

Zone/Habitat: grasslands and pinyon pine/juniper woodlands at 3,000-7,000' (915-2,135 m); hillsides, plains

Range: northeastern and southeastern corners of Arizona, covering two-thirds of the state

Notes: Hardy and drought tolerant, Hartweg Sundrops is often cultivated in rock gardens as ground cover. The masses of blooms on this low-growing evergreen plant attract hawk moths. Flowers open in the afternoon or near sunset and bloom until the next afternoon, when they are replaced by more buds. American Indians used this plant to treat internal bleeding. Found only as far west as Arizona, but ranges eastward to Texas and northward to Kansas.

FLOWER TYPE	LEAF TYPE	LEAF ATTACHMENT	LEAF ATTACHMENT	FRUIT
Regular	Simple	Alternate	Basal	Pod

SUMMER POPPY
Kallstroemia grandiflora

Family: Caltrop (Zygophyllaceae)

Height: 1-4' (30-122 cm)

Flower: round and flat or bowl-shaped orangish yellow flowers, 1-2½" (2.5-6 cm) wide, with dark reddish orange centers, made up of 5 broad fan-shaped petals with dark reddish orange lines and bases; blossoms top long hairy stalks

Leaf: feather-like, dark green leaves, 1-3" (2.5-7.5 cm) long, are divided into 4-8 pairs of elliptical leaflets, opposite on hairy sprawling or erect stems

Bloom: Jul-Oct, after monsoon rains begin

Cycle/Origin: annual; native

Zone/Habitat: desert scrub and grasslands at 1,000-5,000' (305-1,525 m); along roads and sandy washes, flats, slopes, mesas, disturbed areas

Range: southernmost quarter of Arizona and the west central part of the state

Notes: A sprawling annual with orangish yellow flowers on erect hairy stems. Its blooms are sometimes mistaken for the four-petaled flowers of the spring-blooming California Poppy (pg. 341), which is not related. After heavy summer monsoons, this showy flower covers large patches of grasslands and roadsides. Although found in southern California, Summer Poppy is not native there and is common only in southern Arizona, western Texas and northern Mexico.

FLOWER TYPE	LEAF TYPE	LEAF ATTACHMENT
Regular	Compound	Opposite

GOLDEN CROWNBEARD
Verbesina encelioides

Family: Aster (Asteraceae)

Height: 4-20" (10-50 cm)

Flower: layers of 12-15 (or many more) overlapping rectangular petals (ray flowers) with 3-lobed tips surround the wide orange center of this daisy-like yellow flower head, 1½-2" (4-5 cm) wide; each flower is backed by many pointed grayish bracts

Leaf: broadly triangular leaves, ½-6" (3-15 cm) long, are grayish green and have irregular-toothed margins; lower leaves mostly alternate, upper leaves opposite; opposite pairs of smaller, leaf-like appendages (stipules) at base of each leafstalk

Bloom: Mar-Dec

Cycle/Origin: annual; native

Zone/Habitat: desert scrub, grasslands oak/pinyon pine/juniper woodlands below 6,000' (1,830 m); along washes

Range: throughout

Notes: A common annual abundant along roads and in disturbed soils, especially where extra water is found, such as in the floodplains near washes. Eye-catching, bright yellow, daisy-like blooms top this erect plant. "Crownbeard" is for the seed-like fruit topped with gray-brown hairs. Ants, birds and rodents eat the seeds. American Indians used infusions of plant parts to treat skin diseases and spider bites, and drank it as a tea to treat stomach disorders.

FLOWER TYPE	LEAF TYPE	LEAF ATTACHMENT	LEAF ATTACHMENT

Composite   **Simple**   **Alternate**   **Opposite**

BRITTLEBUSH
Encelia farinosa

Family: Aster (Asteraceae)

Height: 1-5' (30-152 cm); shrub

Flower: daisy-like yellow flower head, 1½-2" (4-5 cm) wide, made up of 11-21 lobed petals (ray flowers) around a yellow-to-purplish brown center; groups of flower heads top stalks well above the leaves

Leaf: oval or lance-shaped, bluish green leaves, ¾-3½" (2-9 cm) long, are hairy above with pointed or rounded tips; leaves are clustered near tips of multi-branched whitish stems; stems are covered with matted hairs until older, turning smooth barked

Bloom: Nov-May

Cycle/Origin: perennial; native

Zone/Habitat: desert scrub, grasslands below 3,500' (1,065 m); flats, rocky slopes, along washes

Range: throughout Arizona, except the northeastern and southeastern parts of the state

Notes: Named for its brittle stems, this is usually a mounded bush in full sun, but it can become leggy when shaded or overwatered. The flower heads are borne on thin flower stalks above the grayish green foliage. Drought deciduous, with the leaves turning brown and dropping off during drought; new leaves sprout when it rains. The sap in the stems was burned as incense by early missionaries, thus another common name, Incienso (Spanish for "incense").

"

FLOWER TYPE	LEAF TYPE	LEAF ATTACHMENT
	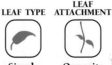	
Composite	Simple	Opposite

SMOOTH DESERT DANDELION
Malacothrix glabrata

Family: Aster (Asteraceae)

Height: 4-16" (10-40 cm)

Flower: yellow and white flower heads, 2" (5 cm) wide, on long stalks; each bloom has no disk flowers, only long narrow petals (ray flowers) tipped with 5 tiny teeth; center is red until all the ray flowers open, then turns dark yellow; outer rim of petals are white

Leaf: basal, dark green, feathery leaves, 2-6" (5-15 cm) long, deeply divided into 3-6 pairs of thread-like lobes with pointed tips

Bloom: Mar-Jun

Cycle/Origin: annual; native

Zone/Habitat: desert scrub below 6,000' (1,830 m); mesas, among creosotebushes and saltbushes, under joshuatrees

Range: western two-thirds of Arizona

Notes: Widespread across the West from Montana to Texas, this low-growing, multi-branching annual grows in sandy or gravelly soils. *Malacothrix* means "soft hair" and refers the usual fuzziness of young plants in this genus, but this species is called *glabrata* for its smoothness and lack of hairs. After heavy winter rains, this wildflower carpets large areas of desert with blooming plants growing in circles similar to fairy rings (mushrooms sprouting around decaying underground material), benefiting baby desert tortoises, which feed on the foliage.

FLOWER TYPE	LEAF TYPE	LEAF ATTACHMENT	LEAF ATTACHMENT
Composite	Simple Lobed	Alternate	Basal

RED DOME BLANKETFLOWER
Gaillardia pinnatifida

Family: Aster (Asteraceae)

Height: 6-16" (15-40 cm)

Flower: yellow flower head, 2" (5 cm) wide, has 5-14 short or long petals (ray flowers) with 3-lobed tips around a fuzzy, domed, dark reddish center (disk flowers)

Leaf: finely hairy basal leaves, 1-2½" (2.5-6 cm) long, are grayish green and lance-shaped to thin; some leaves on each plant have rounded lobes

Bloom: May-Oct

Cycle/Origin: perennial; native

Zone/Habitat: desert scrub, grasslands, oak/pinyon pine/juniper woods, montane at 3,500-7,000' (1,065-2,135 m); plains, mesas, clearings among ponderosa pines

Range: throughout, except the southwestern quarter

Notes: Found from Nevada southeast to Texas and Oklahoma, often along roads. Frequently included in western wildflower seed mixtures, as it grows readily from seed. The basal clump of leaves sends up long slim flower stalks, so the blooms bounce and sway in the wind. The variety found in Arizona has more undivided and narrower leaves than the wider, many-lobed leaves of plants occurring in other states. The genus *Gaillardia* was named after M. Gaillard de Charentonneau, a French magistrate who supported the studies of botanists in the eighteenth century.

FLOWER TYPE	LEAF TYPE	LEAF TYPE	LEAF ATTACHMENT	LEAF ATTACHMENT
		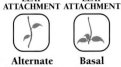		
Composite	Simple	Simple Lobed	Alternate	Basal

DESERT MARIGOLD
Baileya multiradiata

Family: Aster (Asteraceae)

Height: 8-36" (20-91 cm)

Flower: daisy-like, lemon yellow flower head, 2" (5 cm) wide, of multiple layers of 34-55 overlapping petals with tooth-like edges surrounding as many as 100 tiny disk flowers; flower head on long flower stalk

Leaf: rosette of oval, grayish green basal leaves, 1¼-4" (3-10 cm) long, are fuzzy with edges smooth or lobed and resembling the barbs of a feather; stem leaves are much fewer and smaller in the summer

Bloom: Mar-Oct, after rainfall

Cycle/Origin: annual, perennial, biennial; native

Zone/Habitat: desert scrub at 500-5,000' (152-1,525 m); on flats, slopes, along roads, mesas

Range: throughout, except the northwestern corner

Notes: Found only in the Southwest, this is one of the longest-blooming and most common wildflowers in Arizona, often covering hillsides with a yellow haze in spring. Poisonous to sheep and goats, it contains chemicals proven to have anticancer properties. Easily grown from seed, but intolerant of temperatures below 32°F (0°C). In autumn, when Desert Marigold grows smaller flower heads with fewer ray flowers, it is easily confused with Woolly Desert Marigold (*B. pleniradiata*) (not shown), which always has smaller flower heads and fewer ray flowers.

FLOWER TYPE	LEAF TYPE	LEAF ATTACHMENT	LEAF ATTACHMENT
Composite	Simple Lobed	Alternate	Basal

DESERT EVENING-PRIMROSE
Oenothera primiveris

Family: Evening-primrose (Onagraceae)

Height: 4-6" (10-15 cm)

Flower: yellow flower, 2" (5 cm) wide, turns reddish orange when wilted, has 4 broadly heart-shaped petals and 4 hairy, horn-shaped, downward-curving sepals

Leaf: dandelion-like, blunted, lance-shaped green leaves, 1½-11" (4-28 cm) long, coarse-haired, deep irregular lobes; leaves flat or partially erect in basal rosette

Fruit: cylindrical greenish capsules, ½-2½" (1-6 cm) long, sticky red spots, white hairs, 4-winged, open at top

Bloom: middle Feb-May

Cycle/Origin: perennial; native

Zone/Habitat: desert scrub, oak/pinyon pine/juniper woods below 5,300' (1,615 m); sandy flats, rocky slopes, arroyos

Range: northwestern and southern Arizona, ranging over two-thirds of the state

Notes: These low stemless plants have fragrant, pale yellow flowers that are remarkably large compared to the rosette of dandelion-like leaves. Found throughout the Southwest, from southern California to western Texas. Common in the Cabeza Prieta National Wildlife Refuge in southwestern Arizona and along Pantano Wash, near Tucson. Like other evening-primroses, this wildflower opens in the evening; unlike other species, it stays open much of the next day.

FLOWER TYPE	LEAF TYPE	LEAF ATTACHMENT	FRUIT
Regular	Simple Lobed	Basal	Pod

DESERT ROSE MALLOW
Hibiscus coulteri

Family: Mallow (Malvaceae)

Height: 1-4' (30-122 cm); shrub

Flower: bowl-shaped, pale yellow-to-creamy white flowers, 2" (5 cm) wide, have 5 overlapping broad petals with red-streaked bases around a yellow and maroon center; each bloom cupped by 14 thread-like pointed green bracts

Leaf: lower oval and undivided leaves, 1½" (4 cm) long; upper hairy leaves, 1" (2.5 cm) long, have 3 narrow lobes with toothed reddish edges; leaves drop in winter

Fruit: star-shaped tan capsule contains seeds covered with long hairs

Bloom: Feb-Nov, after rain

Cycle/Origin: perennial; native

Zone/Habitat: desert scrub at 1,500-4,500' (460-1,370 m); canyon walls, rocky slopes, limestone soils

Range: southern half of Arizona

Notes: This straggling, sparsely branched shrub is leafy above and woody below. The spindly stems are weak, so it usually grows up through other shrubs for support. The lowest flowers on the stems open first. In the wild, found only in southern Arizona, southern New Mexico, western Texas and northern Mexico. Often cultivated, as it requires little water to keep it blooming most of the year.

FLOWER TYPE	LEAF TYPE	LEAF TYPE	LEAF ATTACHMENT	FRUIT
Regular	Simple	Simple Lobed	Alternate	Pod

DESERT UNICORN PLANT
Proboscidea althaeifolia

Family: Sesame (Pedaliaceae)

Height: 1-2½' (30-76 cm); vine

Flower: yellow tubular flower, 2" (5 cm) long, has orange dotted lines in throat; mouth of tube has 2 lips; upper split and wavy lip bends backward, lower broad bulging lip is horizontal; flowers in groups above the leaves

Leaf: rounded heart-shaped leaves, 1-3" (2.5-7.5 cm) wide, shiny, wrinkled with 3-5 lobes or scalloped edges; long stalks; hairy sticky sprawling stems

Fruit: fuzzy, curved, tapered brown pod, 6" (15 cm) long, opens lengthwise into 2 curving sharp "claws"

Bloom: Jul-Sep

Cycle/Origin: perennial; native

Zone/Habitat: desert scrub below 4,000' (1,220 m); sandy flats, among creosotebushes

Range: southern half of Arizona and the northwestern corner of the state

Notes: This perennial is closely related to the annual Devil's Claw (pg. 241), but has yellow blooms above its shiny leaves instead of white and purple flowers hidden below fuzzy leaves. Both have curved dry claw-like seedpods that attach to the legs of passing animals, dispersing seeds. Desert Unicorn Plant has a thick root that sprouts foliage or flowers only after the monsoons begin.

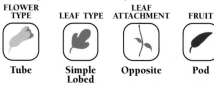

FLOWER TYPE	LEAF TYPE	LEAF ATTACHMENT	FRUIT
Tube	Simple Lobed	Opposite	Pod

ADONIS BLAZING STAR
Mentzelia multiflora

Family: Loasa (Loasaceae)

Height: 6-36" (15-91 cm)

Flower: star-shaped yellow flower, 1½-3" (4-7.5 cm) wide, streaked with orange, has 10 narrow to broad, pointed petals around many long flower parts, with the outer flattened flower parts resembling petals

Leaf: lance-shaped basal leaves, ½-2" (1-15 cm) long, are bluish green, have hook-shaped hairs, variable margins; upper stem leaves much smaller than lower

Fruit: hairy, greenish tan capsule, ⅓-⅔" (.8-1.6 cm) long, cylindrical, cup-shaped at top, tapered base, wick-like center and twisted persistent sepals on edges

Bloom: Apr-Jun

Cycle/Origin: perennial, biennial; native

Zone/Habitat: desert scrub at 100-2,500' (30-760 m); roadsides, along washes, among creosotebushes

Range: throughout

Notes: Adonis Blazing Star flowers open in the late afternoon. One of 23 species of *Mentzelia* in Arizona, most with unusually intricate flowers. The seedpods are as complex as the flowers; each seedpod resembles a candle with a wick in the center, but the top rim is ringed with persistent spider-like sepals. Ranges from southern California to western Texas to southern Wyoming.

FLOWER TYPE	LEAF TYPE	LEAF TYPE	LEAF ATTACHMENT	FRUIT
Regular	Simple	Simple Lobed	Alternate	Pod

ENGELMANN PRICKLY PEAR
Opuntia engelmannii

Family: Cactus (Cactaceae); shrub

Height: 3-10' (.9-3 m)

Flower: cup-shaped flowers, 1½-3½" (4-9 cm) wide, have many overlapping lemon yellow petals around a wide yellow and green center and grow erectly from top edges of flat round stem segments (cactus pads)

Spines: widely spread clusters of 1-6 protruding white spines, ½-1¼" (1-3 cm) long, with reddish flattened bases, red tips; 1 longest spine spreads or points downward; yellowish stiff bristles circle each cluster

Fruit: barrel-shaped, dark red-to-purple pod, 1¼-3½" (3-9 cm) long; smooth, mostly spineless skin; red pulp

Bloom: Apr-May

Cycle/Origin: perennial; native

Zone/Habitat: desert scrub, grassland and oak/pinyon pine/juniper woods at 1,000-5,000' (305-1,525 m); flats, ridges

Range: two-thirds of Arizona, in a band from the northwestern to southeastern parts of the state

Notes: Abundant in southern Arizona, this short-trunked cactus with round or oval, bluish green pads forms a sprawling shrub up to 15 feet (4.6 m) wide. The yellow flowers turn orangish on the second day it blooms. The dark red fruit is edible, thus it is also called Candy Apple. Desert pack rats use the spiny pads to build their mounded nests, forming a protective barrier against predators.

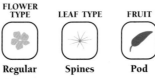

FLOWER TYPE	LEAF TYPE	FRUIT
Regular	Spines	Pod

HAIRY DESERT SUNFLOWER
Geraea canescens

Family: Aster (Asteraceae)

Height: 4-32" (10-80 cm)

Flower: typical yellow sunflower head, 2-3" (5-7.5 cm) wide, has 10-21 oblong 3-lobed petals around a golden orange center; flower heads single or in groups topping the stems well above the leaves

Leaf: hairy, grayish green leaves, ½-4" (1-10 cm) long, are oval or lance-shaped with smooth or toothed edges and pointed tips; lower leaves more numerous and on winged leafstalks; upper leaves stalkless

Bloom: Oct-Jun, but especially common in April

Cycle/Origin: annual; native

Zone/Habitat: desert scrub below 4,500' (1,370 m); along washes

Range: western half of Arizona

Notes: The genus name *Geraea*, from the Greek word for "old," refers to the white-haired leaves, stems, bracts and seeds. Rodents and birds eat the seeds, but enough remain in the soil to produce new plants the following year. This showy sunflower is extremely abundant after heavy rains, and along with Desert Sand Verbena (pg. 167) and Dune Evening-primrose (pg. 247), miles of roadsides and sandy desert flats or valleys are covered with a spectacular display of blooms. Sadly, many desert areas where these beautiful wildflowers once grew are being overrun by the invasive exotic Sahara Mustard (*Brassica tournefortii*) (not shown).

FLOWER TYPE	LEAF TYPE	LEAF ATTACHMENT
Composite	Simple	Alternate

SHOWY GOLDENEYE
Heliomeris multiflora

Family: Aster (Asteraceae)

Height: 12-36" (30-91 cm)

Flower: yellow flower head, 2½" (6 cm) wide, has 8-15 yellow petals (ray flowers) around a darker yellow flat center (disk flowers) that becomes cone-shaped as petals wilt; each bloom held by green bracts

Leaf: long and narrow, stiffly hairy leaves, ¾-2½" (2-6 cm) long, are oppositely attached to branching red stems

Bloom: Jul-Oct

Cycle/Origin: perennial; native

Zone/Habitat: grasslands, oak/pinyon pine/juniper woodlands and montane at 4,500-9,000' (1,370-2,745 m); among ponderosa pines, roadsides, meadows, rocky slopes, upland valleys, disturbed soils

Range: throughout most of Arizona, except in the southwestern corner

Notes: Showy Goldeneye is widespread in the West, especially wherever disturbed soils occur, such as where prairie dogs or gophers dig holes or mounds. Often planted along roads by the state highway department. This showy sunflower is common on the North and South Rims of the Grand Canyon from July through October. Navajo Indians once used the seeds for food and currently use this plant for sheep fodder.

FLOWER TYPE	LEAF TYPE	LEAF ATTACHMENT
Composite	Simple	Opposite

CUTLEAF CONEFLOWER
Rudbeckia laciniata

Family: Aster (Asteraceae)

Height: 5-8' (1.5-2.4 m)

Flower: large yellow flower heads with narrow petals on tall stalks; each coneflower, ¾-5" (2-13 cm) wide, has a cone-shaped green center (disk flowers) surrounded by 8-12 drooping petals (ray flowers)

Leaf: lower leaves, 5-16" (13-40 cm) long, are divided into 3-7 sharp lobes with coarse teeth; upper leaves, 2-3" (5-7.5 cm) long, are simple, coarsely toothed and nearly clasp the stem

Bloom: Jul-Sep

Cycle/Origin: perennial; native

Zone/Habitat: riparian deciduous, montane subalpine at 5,000-8,500' (1,525-2,590 m); meadows, along mountain streams, canyons, rich moist soils

Range: northern half and southeastern corner of Arizona

Notes: A tall and robust perennial, Cutleaf Coneflower grows in moist soils. Look for its green center (cone) and drooping yellow petals, along with the lobed lower leaves and simple upper leaves, to help identify. Often seen growing near streams, in meadows by coniferous forests or in canyon bottoms. A good plant for a butterfly garden. Its flowers attract butterflies such as Monarchs, which drink the nectar. Also known as Green-headed Coneflower or Golden Glow.

FLOWER TYPE	LEAF TYPE	LEAF TYPE	LEAF ATTACHMENT
Composite	Simple	Simple Lobed	Alternate

NODDING SUNFLOWER
Helianthella quinquenervis

Family: Aster (Asteraceae)

Height: 2-5' (61-152 cm)

Flower: composite yellow sunflower, 3" (7.5 cm) wide, has 13-21 slender petals (ray flowers) surrounding a greenish yellow center and is held by sticky fuzzy bracts; drooping flower head found singly or in small groups atop the gray-haired stems

Leaf: wide lance-shaped basal leaves, 4-20" (10-50 cm) long, are grayish green, hairy and have 5 prominent veins; a few opposite stem leaves

Bloom: Jul-Oct

Cycle/Origin: perennial; native

Zone/Habitat: grasslands, montane, subalpine at 5,000-10,000' (1,525-3,050 m); moist meadows, aspen grove and coniferous forest clearings, banks of streams

Range: eastern third of Arizona

Notes: *Helianthella* is Greek for "little sunflower" and *quinquenervis* is Latin for "five-nerved," referring to the veins in the leaves. When ripe, the whole sunflower seed heads are eaten by elk, deer and bears. Compounds in the roots are being investigated for their ability to fight fungal infections. Nectar containing lots of sugar and amino acids is secreted from the bracts of the flower heads and is consumed by ants. The ants, in return, defend the flower against egg-laying flies, whose larvae would eat the developing seeds.

FLOWER TYPE	LEAF TYPE	LEAF ATTACHMENT	LEAF ATTACHMENT
Composite	Simple	Opposite	Basal

GOLDEN COLUMBINE
Aquilegia chrysantha

Family: Buttercup (Ranunculaceae)

Height: 1-4' (30-122 cm)

Flower: large, drooping, bright yellow flower, 3" (7.5 cm) wide, 5 petals and 5 backward-curving, paler yellow sepals; each petal has a hollow nectar-filled spur

Leaf: fern-like, bluish green basal leaves, 3½-18" (9-45 cm) long, divided 2 (can be 3) times into leaflets; each lobed leaflet, 1½" (4 cm) long, is the shape of a piece of pie; stem leaves fewer and smaller

Fruit: green pod, turning brown and papery with age, 1¼-2" (3-5 cm) long, splits along its side to release many shiny round seeds

Bloom: Apr-Sep

Cycle/Origin: perennial; native

Zone/Habitat: riparian deciduous, montane, subalpine at 3,000-11,000' (915-3,355 m); in pine forests, mountains, canyons, seeps, along streams, rich moist soils

Range: throughout, except the southwestern corner

Notes: Genus name *Aquilegia* is from the Latin *aquila*, meaning "eagle" and refers to the five curving spurs that resemble the talons of an eagle. Species name *chrysantha* means "golden flowered." The showy fragrant flowers attract hummingbirds, butterflies, hawk moths and bumblebees to its nectar-filled spurs. The most common and widespread of the seven wild columbines in Arizona.

FLOWER TYPE	LEAF TYPE	LEAF ATTACHMENT	LEAF ATTACHMENT	FRUIT
Irregular	Twice Composite	Alternate	Basal	Pod

HOOKER EVENING-PRIMROSE
Oenothera elata

Family: Evening-primrose (Onagraceae)

Height: 2-8' (.6-2.4 m)

Flower: lemon yellow flower (fading to reddish orange), 3" (7.5 cm) wide, has 4 broad heart-shaped petals and 4 narrow downward-curving sepals

Leaf: lance-shaped to elliptical leaves, 1½-10" (4-25 cm) long, with toothed margins and pointed tips; red stem has sticky hairs with blister-like red bases

Fruit: narrow tapering green pod, ¾-3" (2-7.5 cm) long, turns tan, contains pitted seeds

Bloom: Jul-Oct

Cycle/Origin: biennial; native

Zone/Habitat: pinyon pine/juniper woodlands and montane at 4,000-9,500' (1,220-2,895 m); wet ditches, along roads, clearings among ponderosa pines, moist soils

Range: throughout, except the southwestern corner

Notes: Species name *elata*, which is Latin for "tall," describes this plant well. Found at medium to high elevations, this statuesque plant of coniferous forests has large, bright yellow flowers and bright green leaves growing all along its six (or more) red stems. Forms a basal rosette the first year, sending up the long leafy stalk and blooming during the second. Flowers open in late afternoon, wilting by late morning the next day. The seeds are eaten by finches.

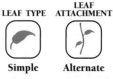

FLOWER TYPE	LEAF TYPE	LEAF ATTACHMENT	FRUIT
Regular	Simple	Alternate	Pod

fruit

MELON LOCO
Apodanthera undulata

Family: Gourd (Cucurbitaceae)

Height: 8-10' (2.4-3 m); vine

Flower: star-shaped yellow flowers, 3-5" (7.5-13 cm) wide, with 5 limp wavy oval petals fused at the bases around a light yellow center; male flowers in loose clusters; larger female blooms are solitary

Leaf: kidney-shaped, dark green leaves, 2-6" (5-15 cm) wide, rough, hairy with lobed or wavy ruffled edges

Fruit: oval or round, hairy hard-shelled melon, 2½-4" (6-10 cm) long, is dark green and turns light green when ripe; has dark ridges that run lengthwise

Bloom: Jun-Sep

Cycle/Origin: perennial; native

Zone/Habitat: desert scrub, grasslands, oak/pinyon pine/juniper woodlands at 1,500-5,500' (460-1,675 m); flats, along roads and washes, floodplains

Range: southeastern quarter of Arizona and the central part of the state

Notes: Can have both male and female flowers, but only develops the female flowers after reaching a certain size. This coarse vine is well adapted to drought, with its large taproot and long large side roots that absorb and store any surface water. Its roots are high in starch. The melon is bitter, but has been eaten during famine. Ranges from Arizona east to Texas and south into northern Mexico.

FLOWER TYPE	LEAF TYPE	LEAF TYPE	LEAF ATTACHMENT	FRUIT
Regular	Simple	Simple Lobed	Alternate	Pod

fruit

BUFFALO GOURD
Cucurbita foetidissima

Family: Gourd (Cucurbitaceae)

Height: 5-20' (1.5-6.1 m); vine

Flower: broad, trumpet-shaped, orange or yellow flowers, 3½-5" (9-13 cm) long; petals flare widely into 5 pointed wrinkled lobes

Leaf: large, heart-shaped, grayish green leaves, 6-12" (15-30 cm) long, have finely toothed edges, are white below, roughly textured and foul smelling

Fruit: gourd-like, resembling a little round watermelon, 3" (7.5 cm) wide, smooth with green and white stripes, then turns all yellow when ripe; pumpkin-like seeds

Bloom: Jul-Sep

Cycle/Origin: perennial; native

Zone/Habitat: desert scrub, grasslands, oak/pinyon pine/juniper woods, montane at 1,000-7,000' (305-2,135 m); along roads and washes, disturbed areas, canyons

Range: northern half and southeastern quarter of Arizona

Notes: Also called Coyote Melon and closely related to garden pumpkins. American Indians have used this plant for 9,000 years, extracting oil for cooking from the edible seeds, or roasting and salting them to eat. Navajos picked the dried fruit to make gourd rattles used during ceremonies. The crushed leaves are an effective insecticide, and the fetid-smelling (thus the species name *foetidissima*) chemicals they contain are being studied for modern uses.

FLOWER TYPE	LEAF TYPE	LEAF ATTACHMENT	FRUIT
	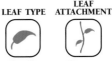		
Tube	Simple	Alternate	Pod

COMMON SUNFLOWER
Helianthus annuus

Family: Aster (Asteraceae)

Height: 3-10' (.9-3 m)

Flower: sunny yellow flower head, 3-6" (7.5-15 cm) wide, with 15-20 yellow petals surrounding a large dark brown or purple center; 2-20 flowers per plant

Leaf: broadly triangular or heart-shaped leaves, 3-12" (7.5-30 cm) long, stiff hairs, coarsely and irregularly toothed; leaves alternate along a very coarse stem

Bloom: Mar-Oct

Cycle/Origin: annual; native

Zone/Habitat: most life zones at 100-7,000' (305-2,135 m); fields, along roads, disturbed ground

Range: throughout

Notes: A smaller, wild version of Giant Sunflower, which is the large cultivated plant often grown in gardens and fields and from which seeds are harvested. Unlike the giant variety, Common Sunflower usually branches several times, but is similar in that it produces many nutritious seeds. Used for food by many peoples historically, the seeds can be ground or pressed to make flour, oil, dyes–even medicine. Often seen growing along highways, where the seeds of maturing plants are dispersed along the road by wind created from passing cars and trucks. Sunflowers do not follow the sun, as is widely believed. Flower heads face the morning sun once the plant matures and begins to bloom, thus most flowers face east.

FLOWER TYPE	LEAF TYPE	LEAF ATTACHMENT
Composite	Simple	Alternate

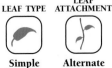

BURROWEED
Isocoma tenuisecta

Family: Aster (Asteraceae)

Height: 12-36" (30-91 cm); shrub

Flower: round clusters, ½-1" (1-2.5 cm) wide, of tiny, disk-shaped, daisy-like, golden yellow flower heads at tips of woody stems; each bloom has only disk flowers (no ray flowers)

Leaf: stiffly upright, sticky, dark green leaves, 1-1½" (2.5-4 cm) long, are deeply divided into 4-8 short slim lobes with sharply pointed tips

Bloom: Sep-Nov

Cycle/Origin: perennial; native

Zone/Habitat: desert scrub, grasslands, oak/pinyon pine/juniper woodlands at 2,000-6,500' (610-1,980 m); dry slopes, along roads, disturbed areas, scattered on rangelands, among creosotebushes

Range: southeastern two-thirds of Arizona, especially around Tucson

Notes: Forms rounded, semi-woody bushes topped with yellow blooms that turn tan when dry and remain on the plant. Becoming common in landscaping. The foliage is toxic if eaten by livestock, particularly horses. Cows grazing on Burroweed produce milk containing tremetol, a chemical poisonous to people. Will become invasive in overgrazed pastures. Occurs in the wild only in Arizona and New Mexico in the U.S. and in northern Mexico.

CLUSTER TYPE	FLOWER TYPE	LEAF TYPE	LEAF ATTACHMENT
		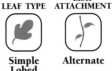	
Round	**Composite**	**Simple Lobed**	**Alternate**

NEW MEXICO GROUNDSEL
Packera neomexicana

Family: Aster (Asteraceae)

Height: 8-20" (20-50 cm)

Flower: yellow, relatively flat cluster, 1-2" (2.5-5 cm) wide, of 3-20 composite flower heads, each 1" (2.5 cm) wide, made up of 5-8 (sometimes 13) petals surrounding a darker yellow center; cluster is shaped like an open umbrella

Leaf: oval to narrowly lance-shaped basal leaves, ¾-2½" (2-6 cm) long, with woolly hairs, variable margins; the few stem leaves are smaller going up the stem

Bloom: Apr-Aug

Cycle/Origin: perennial; native

Zone/Habitat: interior chaparral, montane and subalpine at 3,000-9,000' (915-2,745 m); dry hillsides, meadows

Range: throughout, except the southwestern corner

Notes: The most common of the ten species of *Packera* in Arizona. These species are often called DYCs for "darn yellow composites," since they are so difficult to distinguish from each other as the result of hybridization. Also called New Mexico Butterweed for the buttery color of the flowers, which are loosely grouped or in dense clusters at the top of the branching flower stalk. The tall, almost leafless flower stalk is typical of this plant. The basal rosette's density and number of leaves depends on the amount of rainfall where the plant grows.

CLUSTER TYPE	FLOWER TYPE	LEAF TYPE	LEAF TYPE	LEAF ATTACHMENT	LEAF ATTACHMENT
Flat	Composite	Simple	Simple Lobed	Alternate	Basal

395

MOUNTAIN PARSLEY
Pseudocymopterus montanus

Family: Carrot (Apiaceae)

Height: 10-24" (25-61 cm)

Flower: small clusters (umbels) of tiny flowers forming larger, golden yellow-to-orangish red flat clusters, 1-3" (2.5-7.5 cm) wide

Leaf: extremely variable leaves (can be lobed, compound or twice compound), 2-6" (5-15 cm) long, are finely divided into leaflets of various sizes and shapes

Fruit: oblong ridged green capsule, $\frac{1}{4}$" (.6 cm) long, turns bright red when mature

Bloom: May-Oct

Cycle/Origin: perennial; native

Zone/Habitat: grasslands, montane, subalpine at 5,500-11,500' (1,675-3,510 m); meadows, aspen groves

Range: northern half and southeastern corner of Arizona

Notes: The height, leaves and flowers of Mountain Parsley are highly variable. The odorous leaves are sometimes feather-like and differ in how many times they are divided. The leaflets vary greatly in size and shape, from wide and lobed to narrow with smooth edges. Interestingly, the flowers can vary from golden yellow to orangish red on the same plant. A member of the Carrot family, which includes plants with hollow stems such as common garden parsley, carrot and dill. Also called Alpine False Spring Parsley.

CLUSTER TYPE	FLOWER TYPE	LEAF TYPE	LEAF TYPE	LEAF ATTACHMENT	FRUIT
Flat	Regular	Simple Lobed	Twice Compound	Basal	Pod

397

WESTERN WALLFLOWER
Erysimum capitatum

Family: Mustard (Brassicaceae)

Height: 12-32" (30-80 cm)

Flower: many small yellow-to-orange flowers, ¾" (2 cm) wide, in a nearly round or cylindrical cluster, 1½-3½" (4-11 cm) wide; each flower has 4 oval petals, protruding green flower parts and long green sepals (calyx); cluster blooms from the bottom up

Leaf: basal rosette of narrowly lance-shaped leaves; 1-5" (2.5-13 cm) long, have pointed tips and are on short stalks; erect stem leaves are stalkless

Fruit: erect pod-like green container, turning brown, 2-4" (5-10 cm) long, has 4 sides, is long, thin and fleshy

Bloom: Mar-Sep

Cycle/Origin: perennial, biennial; native

Zone/Habitat: all life zones above 2,500' (760 m); slopes, canyons

Range: throughout, except the southwestern corner

Notes: The name "Wallflower" comes from a close relative from Eurasia that is often found growing on stone walls. The species name *capitatum* is Latin for "head" and refers to the head-shaped cluster of flowers. In coniferous forests above 7,000 feet (2,135 m), the flowers of this very common native mustard are orange. This orange variety was once considered a separate species, but it is now thought that Western Wallflower is just an extremely variable plant.

CLUSTER TYPE	FLOWER TYPE	LEAF TYPE	LEAF ATTACHMENT	LEAF ATTACHMENT	FRUIT
Round	Regular	Simple	Alternate	Basal	Pod

TURPENTINEBUSH
Ericameria laricifolia

Family: Aster (Asteraceae)

Height: 12-36" (30-91 cm); shrub

Flower: daisy-like yellow flower heads, each ⅜" (.9 cm) wide, with 3-6 petals and a ragged yellow-orange center; flowers form a dense flat cluster, 3" (7.5 cm) wide; highest cluster on the plant blooms first

Leaf: needle-like, leathery, grayish green leaves, ½-1½" (1-4 cm) long, are erect and sticky; erect, nearly parallel branches grow closely together

Bloom: Aug-Dec

Cycle/Origin: perennial; native

Zone/Habitat: desert scrub, pinyon pine/juniper woods at 3,000-6,000' (915-1,830 m); canyons, creosotebush flats, mountain slopes, rocky cliffs, mesas

Range: southern half and northwestern quarter of Arizona

Notes: The stems and leaves, when crushed, exude a resin that smells like turpentine, thus part of the plant's common name. Turpentinebush is a showy bloomer covering hillsides with yellow masses in the fall. It retains the fluffy, dandelion-like, tan flower parts through the winter. This low-growing evergreen shrub forms a compact mound that needs no trimming and is attractive in desert landscaping, even when not in bloom. Cultivated varieties can be seen on highway medians. Tolerates heat and cold to down to 32°F (0°C), while requiring little water once established.

CLUSTER TYPE	FLOWER TYPE	LEAF TYPE	LEAF ATTACHMENT
			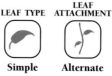
Flat	Composite	Simple	Alternate

YELLOW SWEET CLOVER
Melilotus officinalis

Family: Pea or Bean (Fabaceae)

Height: 3-6' (.9-1.8 m)

Flower: spike cluster, 1½-5" (4-13 cm) long, of yellow flowers; each flower is ¼" (.6 cm) long

Leaf: each leaf is made up of 3 narrow, toothed, lance-shaped leaflets, ½-1" (1-2.5 cm) long; leaves are alternately attached to branching stem

Fruit: egg-shaped flattened green pod, turning brown, ¼" (.6 cm) long

Bloom: Jun-Aug

Cycle/Origin: annual, biennial; non-native

Zone/Habitat: all life zones below 7,500' (2,285 m); in agricultural areas, roadsides, along railroads, open fields, waste areas

Range: eastern two-thirds of Arizona

Notes: This non-native plant was introduced from Europe via Eurasia. Once grown as a hay crop, it has escaped cultivation and now grows throughout Arizona along roads and fields. When crushed, the leaves and flowers smell like vanilla. Appropriately in the genus *Melilotus*, which is Greek for "honey," as bees produce honey from the nectar of this plant. The leaves are eaten by white-tailed and mule deer. The rodenticide warfarin was developed from the chemical dicoumarin, which is found in sweet clover.

CLUSTER TYPE	FLOWER TYPE	LEAF TYPE	LEAF ATTACHMENT	LEAF ATTACHMENT	FRUIT
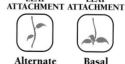					
Spike	Irregular	Compound	Alternate	Basal	Pod

SCRAMBLED EGGS
Corydalis aurea

Family: Fumitory (Fumariaceae)

Height: 8-12" (20-30 cm)

Flower: irregularly shaped, tubular yellow flowers, ¾" (2 cm) long, attached horizontally in spike clusters, 3-4" (7.5-10 cm) long; each bloom has 4 fused petals; top petal forms a hood and a broad, hollow, downward-curving spur; bottom fringed petal is lip-like and drooping

Leaf: feathery, bluish green leaves, 3-6" (7.5-15 cm) long, with pairs of lobed leaflets; reddish green stems

Fruit: thin curved flattened seedpods, 1" (2.5 cm) long

Bloom: Feb-Jun

Cycle/Origin: annual, biennial; native

Zone/Habitat: desert scrub, grasslands, oak/pinyon pine/juniper woodlands and montane at 1,500-9,000' (460-2,745 m); disturbed areas, along washes, old fields

Range: throughout, except the southwestern corner

Notes: The Navajo Indians used this plant medicinally for various ailments and as a disinfectant. Contains toxic alkaloids. Each of the seeds has a nutritious blob attached that ants consume, but contains chemicals that repel mice. The ants collect the seeds and store them below ground, where the seeds remain after the ants eat the blob. This protects the seeds from wildfires and mice, which are kept out of the ant colonies by the soldier ants.

CLUSTER TYPE	FLOWER TYPE	LEAF TYPE	LEAF ATTACHMENT	FRUIT
Spike	Irregular	Compound	Alternate	Pod

TRANSPECOS THIMBLEHEAD
Hymenothrix wislizeni

Family: Aster (Asteraceae)

Height: 12-28" (30-71 cm)

Flower: flat-topped, branched, orangish yellow cluster, 2-6" (5-15 cm) wide, of many small flower heads; each flower head has 3-8 narrow toothed yellow petals (ray flowers) around a yellow center of 15-30 disk flowers; several clusters per plant

Leaf: leaves are divided into 3 narrow, irregular-shaped lobes; each leaf, 1-5" (2.5-13 cm) long, is alternately attached to a branched stem; most of the leaves are near the base; the upper leaves are much smaller

Bloom: Jun-Dec

Cycle/Origin: annual, biennial; native

Zone/Habitat: desert scrub and grasslands at 2,000-5,000' (600-1,500 m); along roads and washes, slopes

Range: southern half of Arizona, except the southwestern edge of the state

Notes: "Transpecos" is the region in western Texas near the Pecos River, where this plant was first found. "Thimblehead" is for the resemblance of its unopened flower head buds to a sewing thimble. This common roadside weed is also called Wislizenus Beeflower for the powerful attraction of its flowers to bees. There are more than 1,000 different species of wild bees found near Tucson. The foliage of this wildflower is eaten by javelinas (pig-like animals).

CLUSTER TYPE	FLOWER TYPE	LEAF TYPE	LEAF ATTACHMENT
Flat	Composite	Simple Lobed	Alternate

leaf cluster

SMOOTH GOLDENROD
Solidago missouriensis

Family: Aster (Asteraceae)

Height: 12-36" (30-91 cm)

Flower: golden yellow clusters, 3-6" (7.5-15 cm) long, of many tiny, daisy-like flower heads, ¼" (.6 cm) wide; each bloom has 5-14 petals (ray flowers) around a yellow center

Leaf: lance-shaped, shiny and smooth, dark green leaves, 2-6" (5-15 cm) long, with smooth edges that curl upward; upper leaves are shorter and narrow; a few tiny leaves cluster in each leaf junction (axis); leaves alternate along the reddish smooth stem

Bloom: Jun-Aug

Cycle/Origin: perennial; native

Zone/Habitat: grasslands, oak/pinyon pine/juniper woods, montane at 5,000-9,000' (1,525-2,745 m); open forests

Range: throughout, except the southwestern corner

Notes: "Goldenrod" is an apt description for this upright narrow plant topped with bright yellow flower clusters. One of nine species of *Solidago* in Arizona, but Smooth Goldenrod is distinguished by the tiny leaf clusters in each leaf axis (see inset). Grows in large clumps, sending up numerous branchless stems from spreading underground runners. American Indians chewed the roots to ease toothaches. Widespread in most of the West and Midwest, decorating areas along highways and railroads in late summer.

CLUSTER TYPE	FLOWER TYPE	LEAF TYPE	LEAF ATTACHMENT
Spike	Composite	Simple	Alternate

YELLOW OWL'S CLOVER
Orthocarpus luteus

Family: Snapdragon (Scrophulariaceae)

Height: 4-16" (10-40 cm)

Flower: spike clusters, 2-8" (5-20 cm) long, of 2-lipped yellow flowers, ½" (1 cm) long; flowers are partially hidden by conspicuous, 3-lobed, purplish green bracts covered with sticky, glistening white hairs

Leaf: narrow dark green leaves, ½-2" (1-5 cm) long, have smooth edges; upper leaves have 3 lobes; alternately attached, spiraling up the stem

Fruit: straight-sided tan pods, ¼" (.6 cm) long

Bloom: Jul-Sep

Cycle/Origin: annual; native

Zone/Habitat: higher oak/pinyon pine/juniper woodlands, montane, subalpine at 7,000-9,500' (2,135-2,895 m); among coniferous trees, moist meadows, in sagebrush scrub, slopes

Range: northern half of Arizona

Notes: *Orthocarpus* means "straight fruit" in Greek, referring to the seedpods. Famous botanist Thomas Nuttall collected this annual in North Dakota in the early 1800s and named the genus. The small roots of this semiparasitic plant invade the roots of other plants to obtain part of their nutrition. This slender leafy plant is the most widespread of owl's clover, ranging to California, Washington, western Minnesota and New Mexico.

CLUSTER TYPE	FLOWER TYPE	LEAF TYPE	LEAF TYPE	LEAF ATTACHMENT	FRUIT
Spike	Irregular	Simple	Simple Lobed	Alternate	Pod

BROOM RAGWORT
Senecio spartioides

Family: Aster (Asteraceae)

Height: ½-3½' (15-107 cm); shrub

Flower: flat-topped yellow clusters, 4-8" (10-20 cm) wide, of 10-20 daisy-like flower heads, ¾" (2 cm) wide; each bloom has 4-8 slightly drooping, non-overlapping, narrow yellow petals with double-notched tips, surrounding a small orange center

Leaf: narrow and long or thread-like, bright green leaves, 2-4" (5-10 cm) long, are smooth with smooth edges; lower leaves die before flowers open

Bloom: Jul-Oct

Cycle/Origin: perennial; native

Zone/Habitat: grasslands, oak/pinyon pine/juniper woodlands, montane at 6,500-9,000' (1,980-2,745 m); open disturbed or sandy areas, along streams, canyons

Range: throughout

Notes: This airy, bright green shrub has many multi-branched stems with lots of yellow flower heads in wide flat clusters. The lower leaves wither and fall off by the time the plant blooms, making it appear dead below. It is abundant during late summer in northern Arizona, where it grows in rocky high-elevation grasslands, forming large colonies among the grasses. Threadleaf Ragwort (pg. 339) is similar to Broom Ragwort, but is overall hairy and has divided leaves.

CLUSTER TYPE	FLOWER TYPE	LEAF TYPE	LEAF ATTACHMENT
		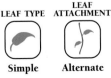	
Flat	Composite	Simple	Alternate

FIDDLENECK
Amsinckia menziesii

Family: Forget-me-not (Boraginaceae)

Height: 8-20" (20-50 cm)

Flower: yellow-to-yellowish orange flowers in a coiled spike cluster, 8" (20 cm) long; each trumpet-shaped flower is ⅙-½" (.4-1 cm) long and has a reddish orange throat; buds and stems are covered with fine white hairs

Leaf: basal leaves, 1-6" (2.5-15 cm) long, are narrowly lance-shaped, dark green and stalkless; stem leaves are gradually shorter farther up the stem; prickly white hairs cover the stems and leaves

Fruit: greenish red pod, turning brown, ⅝-1" (1.5-2.5 cm) long, is bean-like, slender and flattened

Bloom: Mar-May

Cycle/Origin: annual; native

Zone/Habitat: desert scrub, grasslands below 4,000' (1,220 m); disturbed areas, along washes and roads, flats

Range: throughout Arizona, except the northeastern corner

Notes: The common name refers to the resemblance of the flower spike to the neck of a violin, which is also coiled at its end. The bright flowers open first at the top of the coil, which gradually straightens as the lower flowers open. Large fallow fields sometimes contain many Fiddlenecks; grazing cows avoid eating the plants since they contain alkaloids poisonous to livestock.

CLUSTER TYPE	FLOWER TYPE	LEAF TYPE	LEAF ATTACHMENT	LEAF ATTACHMENT
Spike	Tube	Simple	Alternate	Basal

GOLDENPEA
Thermopsis montana

Family: Pea or Bean (Fabaceae)

Height: 24-36" (61-91 cm)

Flower: dense spike cluster, 5-12" (13-30 cm) long, of large, pea-like, bright yellow flowers, 1" (2.5 cm) long

Leaf: bright green leaves, 8" (20 cm) long, divided into 3 oval leaflets, 4" (10 cm) long, with pointed tips, prominent central veins, smooth edges; pairs of small appendages (stipules) at bases of leafstalks

Fruit: straight flattened bean-like pod, 3" (7.5 cm) long, is stalkless, erect and fuzzy green, turning smooth and tan when mature

Bloom: Apr-Jul

Cycle/Origin: perennial; native

Zone/Habitat: montane and subalpine at 6,000-11,000' (1,830-3,355 m); in openings among coniferous trees, in moist soils

Range: northern half of Arizona

Notes: This conspicuous flower spreads by underground roots, sending up stems at closely spaced intervals and forming colonies of plants as tall as 2-3 feet (61-91 cm). The large, pea-like flowers are shaped like lupine blooms, thus the genus name *Thermopsis,* from the Greek *thermos* for "lupine" and *opsis* for "similar." The foliage is avoided by livestock, but it is required food for caterpillars of the large and showy Queen Alexandra Sulphur butterfly.

CLUSTER TYPE	FLOWER TYPE	LEAF TYPE	LEAF ATTACHMENT	FRUIT
Spike	Irregular	Compound	Alternate	Pod

COMMON MULLEIN
Verbascum thapsus

Family: Snapdragon (Scrophulariaceae)

Height: 2-6' (.6-1.8 m)

Flower: club-like spike cluster, 12-24" (30-61 cm) long, of many small yellow flowers packed along the stalk, opening only a few at a time, from the top down; each flower, ¾-1" (2-2.5 cm) wide, has 5 petals

Leaf: large basal leaves, 12-15" (30-38 cm) long, are velvety with a thick covering of stiff hairs; stalkless upper leaves clasp main stem at alternate intervals; leaves are progressively smaller toward top of stalk

Bloom: Jun-Sep

Cycle/Origin: biennial; non-native

Zone/Habitat: oak/pinyon pine/juniper woodlands and montane at 5,000-7,000' (1,525-2,135 m); disturbed sites

Range: northern half and southeastern corner of Arizona

Notes: A European import known for its very soft, flannel-like leaves, hence its other common name, Flannel Plant. This biennial takes two years to mature. The first year it grows as a low rosette of large soft leaves; in the second, a tall flower stalk sprouts. Its dried stems stand well into winter. It is said the Romans dipped its dried flower stalks in animal tallow to use as torches. Victorian women rubbed the leaves on their cheeks, slightly irritating their skin, to add a dash of blush. Early settlers and American Indians placed the soft woolly leaves in footwear for warmth and comfort.

CLUSTER TYPE	FLOWER TYPE	LEAF TYPE	LEAF ATTACHMENT	LEAF ATTACHMENT	LEAF ATTACHMENT

Spike	Regular	Simple	Alternate	Clasping	Basal

GLOSSARY

Alternate: A type of leaf attachment in which the leaves are singly and alternately attached along a stem, not paired or in whorls.

Annual: A plant that germinates, flowers and sets seed during a single growing season and returns the following year from seed only.

Anther: A part of the male flower that contains the pollen.

Arroyo: A usually dry and sandy streambed in the Southwest over which water flows during or after heavy rains. See *wash*.

Axis: A point on the main stem from which lateral branches arise.

Basal: The leaves at the base of a plant near the ground, usually grouped in a round rosette.

Bell flower: A single, downward-hanging flower that has petals fused together, forming a bell-like shape. See *tube flower*.

Berry: A fleshy fruit that contains one or many seeds.

Biennial: A plant that lives for two years, blooming in the second year.

Bract: A leaf-like structure usually found at the base of a flower, often appearing as a petal.

Bulb: A short, round, underground shoot that is used as a food storage system, common in the Lily family.

Calyx: A collective group of all of the sepals of a flower.

Capsule: A pod-like fruiting structure that contains many seeds and has more than one chamber. See *pod*.

Cauline: The leaves that attach to the stem distinctly above the ground, as opposed to basal leaves, which attach near the ground.

Clasping: A type of leaf attachment in which the leaf base partly surrounds the main stem of the plant at the point of attachment; grasping the stem without a leafstalk.

Cluster: A group or collection of flowers or leaves.

Composite flower: A collection of tiny or small flowers that appears as one large flower, usually made up of ray and disk flowers, common in the Aster family.

Compound leaf: A single leaf composed of a central stalk and two or more leaflets.

Corolla: All of the petals of a flower that fuse together to form a tube.

Creosotebush: A yellow-flowered evergreen bush with a resinous odor, most strongly fragrant after rainfall, abundant in Southwest deserts.

Disk flower: One of many small, tubular flowers in the central part (disk) of a composite flower, common in the Aster family.

Ephemeral: Lasting for only a short time each spring.

Flat cluster: A group of flowers that forms a flat-topped structure, which allows flying insects to easily land and complete pollination.

Gland: A tiny structure that usually secretes oil or nectar, sometimes found on leaves, stems, stalks and flowers, as in Curlycup Gumweed.

Globular: Having a spherical or globe-like shape.

Irregular flower: A flower that does not have the typical round shape, usually made up of five or more petals that are fused together in an irregular shape, common in the Pea or Bean family.

Keel: The two lower petals, often fused together, of a flower in the Pea or Bean family.

Leaflet: One of two or more leaf-like parts of a compound leaf.

Lip: The projection of a flower petal or the "odd" petal, such as the large inflated petal common in the Snapdragon family; sometimes, the lobes of a petal. See *lobe*.

Lobe: A large rounded projection of a petal or leaf, larger than the tooth of a leaf.

Lobed leaf: A simple leaf with at least one indentation (sinus) along an edge that does not reach the center or base of the leaf, as in Common Dandelion.

Margin: The edge of a leaf.

Mesa: An elevated, flat expanse of land (plateau), with one or more steep sides or cliffs; Spanish for "tableland."

Node: The place or point of origin on a stem where leaves attach or have been attached.

Nutlet: A small or diminutive nut or seed.

Opposite: A type of leaf attachment in which the leaves are situated directly across from each other on a stem.

Palmate leaf: A type of compound leaf in which three or more leaflets arise from a common central point at the end of a leafstalk, as in Arroyo Lupine.

Parasitic: A plant or fungus that derives its food or water chiefly from another plant, to the detriment of the host plant. See *semiparasitic*.

Perennial: A plant that lives from several to many seasons, returning each year from its roots.

Perfoliate: A type of leaf attachment in which the bases of at least two leaves connect around the main stem so that the stem appears to pass through one stalkless leaf.

Petal: A basic flower part that is usually brightly colored, serving to attract pollinating insects.

Photosynthesis: In green plants, the conversion of water and carbon dioxide into carbohydrates (food) from the energy in sunlight.

Pistil: The female part of a flower made up of an ovary, style and stigma, often in the center of the flower.

Playa: The flat bottom of a desert valley, temporarily covered with water after heavy rains.

Pod: A dry fruiting structure that contains many seeds, often with a single chamber. See *capsule*.

Pollination: The transfer of pollen from the male anther to the female stigma, usually resulting in the production of seeds.

Radial spine: One of the outermost spines of a cluster, radiating from the longer central spines, spreading and pressed flat against the stem, as in cacti.

Ray flower: One of many individual outer flowers of a composite flower, common in the Aster family.

Recurved: Curved backward or downward, as in bracts or sepals.

Regular flower: A flower with 3 to 20 typical petals that are arranged in a circle.

Rhizome: A creeping, (usually) horizontal, underground stem.

Rosette: A cluster of leaves arranged in a circle, often at the base of the plant, as in Common Mullein.

Round cluster: A group of many flowers that forms a round structure, giving the appearance of one large flower.

Seed head: A group or cluster of seeds

Semiparasitic: A type of plant or fungus that derives a portion, but not all, of its food or water chiefly from another plant, to the detriment of the host plant. See *parasitic*.

Sepal: A member of the outermost set of petals of a flower, typically green or leafy, but often colored and resembling a petal.

Simple leaf: A single leaf with an undivided or unlobed edge.

Spike cluster: A group of many flowers on a single, spike-like stem, giving the appearance of one large flower.

Spine: A modified leaf; a stiff, usually short, sharply pointed outgrowth. See *thorn*.

Spur: A hollow, tube-like appendage of a flower, usually where nectar is located, as in Golden Columbine.

Stamen: The male parts of a flower, consisting of a filament and an anther.

Standard: The uppermost petal of a flower in the Pea or Bean family.

Stem leaf: Any leaf that grows along the stem of a plant, as opposed to a leaf at the base of a plant. See *cauline* and *basal*.

Stigma: The female part of the flower that receives the pollen.

Stipule: A basal appendage (usually in pairs) of a leaf that is not attached to the leaf blade, as in Goldenpea.

Taproot: The primary, vertically descending root of a plant.

Tendril: A twining, string-like structure of a vine that clings to plants or other objects for support.

Terminal: Growing at the end of a leaf, stem or stalk.

Thorn: A modified part of a stem; a stiff, usually long and sharply pointed outgrowth. See *spine*.

Throat: The opening or orifice of a tubular flower (corolla or calyx).

Toothed: Having a jagged or serrated edge of a leaf, resembling teeth of a saw.

Tube flower: A flower with fused petals forming a tube and usually turned upward. See *bell flower*.

Umbel: A domed to relatively flat-topped flower cluster that resembles the overall shape of an open umbrella, common in the Carrot family.

Wash: A usually dry and sandy streambed in the Southwest over which water flows during or after heavy rains. See *arroyo*.

Whorled: A type of attachment in which a circle or ring of three or more similar leaves, stems or flowers originate from a common point.

Wing: A flat extension at the base of a leaf or edge of a leafstalk, sometimes extending down the stem of the plant; one of the side petals of a flower, common in the Pea or Bean family.

Woody: Having the appearance or texture resembling wood, as in stems, bark or taproots.

☐ Agoseris, Pale 343

☐ Alfalfa 161

☐ Anemone, Desert............239

☐ Aster, Hoary Tansy-........145

☐ Aster, Lacy Tansy- 323

☐ Aster, Tansyleaf Tansy- ..143

☐ Barrel, Fishhook 61

☐ Beeblossom, Scarlet........115

☐ Bee Plant,
    Rocky Mountain 171

☐ Beloperone......................189

☐ Bergamot, Wild 159

☐ Bindweed, Field 243

☐ Bladderpod, Gordon 305

☐ Blanketflower,
    Red Dome 361

☐ Blazing Star, Adonis........371

☐ Bluebells, Franciscan......23

☐ Brittlebush......................357

☐ Brittlebush, Button 313

☐ Buckwheat,
    Eastern Mojave 109

☐ Buffalo Gourd 389

☐ Burroweed......................393

☐ Butterflyweed 67

☐ Camphorweed................315

☐ Cardinalflower................205

☐ Cassia, Coves..................331

☐ Catchfly, Cardinal 183

☐ Chia................................37

☐ Chicory, Desert 235

☐ Cholla, Staghorn 181

☐ Cinchweed,
    Many-bristled 289

☐ Cinquefoil, Scarlet..........179

☐ Clammyweed,
    Red Whisker 279

☐ Clematis,
    Western White 281

☐ Clover, Owl's 175

☐ Clover, Scruffy Prairie 263

☐ Clover, Yellow Owl's 411

☐ Clover, Yellow Sweet 403

☐ Columbine, Golden........383

☐ Coneflower, Cutleaf........379

☐ Coneflower,
    Upright Prairie................327

☐ Coralbells 113

☐ Coralbells, Pink..............119

☐ Cream Cup 221

☐ Cress, Alpine Penny 265

☐ Crownbeard, Golden......355

☐ Daisy, Angelita 347

☐ Daisy, Blackfoot 231

☐ Daisy, Emory Rock 209

☐ Daisy,
Stemless Townsend 237

☐ Dandelion, Common......345

☐ Dandelion, Smooth
Desert 359

☐ Datura, Sacred................253

☐ Dayflower, Bird's Bill 27

☐ Deervetch, Foothill 287

☐ Deervetch, Shrubby........311

☐ Deervetch, Wright 293

☐ Desert-honeysuckle,
Thurber 57

☐ Devil's Claw 241

☐ Dock, Canaigre 51

☐ Dogbane, Spreading 75

☐ Dogweed 297

☐ Elkweed 53

☐ Evening-primrose,
Desert 365

☐ Evening-primrose,
Dune 247

☐ Evening-primrose,
Hooker 385

☐ Evening-primrose,
Tufted 249

☐ Fairy Duster....................105

☐ Fanpetals, Spreading 319

☐ Fiddleneck......................415

☐ Filaree 101

☐ Firecrackerbush..............187

☐ Five Eyes, Greenleaf 303

☐ Five Spot, Desert 85

☐ Flax, Western Blue 35

☐ Fleabane, Spreading 233

☐ Four O'clock,
Colorado 147

☐ Four O'clock, Trailing 83

☐ Garlic, Texas False..........211

☐ Gentian, Pleated 141

☐ Geranium, Pineywoods 79

☐ Geranium, Richardson ..223

☐ Ghostflower....................333

☐ Gilia, Long-flowered 31

☐ Gilia, Scarlet 203

☐ Goldeneye, Showy..........377

☐ Goldenpea......................417

☐ Goldenrod, Smooth........409

☐ Groundsel,
New Mexico 395

☐ Gumweed, Curlycup......337

☐ Hedgehog,
Pink-flowered 99

☐ Hedge-nettle, Scarlet 199

426

☐ Hibiscus, Rock.................87
☐ Honeysuckle, Arizona 55
☐ Honeysuckle, Thurber
Desert-............................57
☐ Hummingbird's
Trumpet.........................59
☐ Hyacinth, Wild 139
☐ Hymenopappus,
Fineleaf 325
☐ Indian Blanket 63
☐ Iris, Rocky Mountain......151
☐ Janusia, Slender.............291
☐ Larkspur, Barestem 45
☐ Larkspur, Desert 47
☐ Lettuce,
Brown-plumed Wire 133
☐ Lily, Desert....................285
☐ Lily, Desert Mariposa........65
☐ Lily, Doubting
Mariposa 245
☐ Lupine, Arroyo 43
☐ Lupine, Bajada 39
☐ Lupine, Blue Bonnet 41
☐ Mallow, Caliche Globe......69
☐ Mallow, Desert Globe 71
☐ Mallow, Desert Rose 367
☐ Mallow, Hoary Indian 309

☐ Mallow,
New Mexico Checker 117
☐ Mallow,
Small-flowered Globe 73
☐ Marigold, Desert 363
☐ Melon Loco 387
☐ Milkvetch, Arizona 111
☐ Milkvetch,
Small-flowered 127
☐ Milkweed, Poison 259
☐ Milkweed, Spider 271
☐ Mint, Wild....................103
☐ Monkeyflower,
Cardinal.........................191
☐ Monkeyflower, Seep 317
☐ Monkshood,
Columbian......................49
☐ Morning Glory,
Arizona 25
☐ Morning Glory,
Bird's Foot 95
☐ Morning Glory, Ivyleaf......29
☐ Morning Glory, Tall 149
☐ Mullein, Common..........419
☐ Nama, Bristly.................129
☐ Nettle, Scarlet Hedge- 199
☐ Nightshade, Silverleaf 137

427

☐ Onion, Nodding 157
☐ Paintbrush,
   Desert Indian.................197
☐ Paintbrush,
   Woolly Indian 195
☐ Paperflower,
   Whitestem....................321
☐ Parsley, Mountain 397
☐ Pea, Grassleaf............169
☐ Penstemon, Beardlip 201
☐ Penstemon, Desert..........121
☐ Penstemon, Firecracker..193
☐ Penstemon, Palmer 125
☐ Penstemon, Parry 123
☐ Phacelia, Blue 153
☐ Pincushion,
   Arizona Fishhook 89
☐ Pincushion, Desert 225
☐ Plantain, Woolly 273
☐ Plume, Apache 227
☐ Plume, Feather 163
☐ Popcornflower, Arizona..261
☐ Popcornflower,
   Narrowleaf....................275
☐ Poppy, California...........341
☐ Poppy,
   Southwestern Prickly 251

☐ Poppy, Summer 353
☐ Prickly Pear,
   Engelmann 373
☐ Primrose,
   Desert Evening-............365
☐ Primrose,
   Dune Evening- 247
☐ Primrose,
   Hooker Evening-............385
☐ Primrose,
   Tufted Evening-..............249
☐ Puccoon,
   Many-flowered 295
☐ Pussytoes,
   Rocky Mountain 255
☐ Ragwort, Broom 413
☐ Ragwort, Threadleaf 339
☐ Ratany, Littleleaf...............81
☐ Rose, Arizona 91
☐ Sandmat, Whitemargin ..207
☐ Sandwort, Fendler..........219
☐ Scrambled Eggs..............405
☐ Shepherd's Purse 283
☐ Snakeroot, Fragrant........267
☐ Snapdragonvine..............131
☐ Solomon's Seal, False......277
☐ Sow-thistle, Spiny 329

☐ Spiderwort, Prairie 33
☐ Strawberry, Wild 213
☐ Suncup, California 307
☐ Sundrops, Hartweg 351
☐ Sunflower, Common 391
☐ Sunflower,
Hairy Desert 375
☐ Sunflower, Nodding 381
☐ Sweetbush 299
☐ Tansy-aster, Hoary..........145
☐ Tansy-aster, Lacy 323
☐ Tansy-aster, Tansyleaf 143
☐ Thimblehead,
Transpecos......................407
☐ Thistle, Arizona 185
☐ Thistle, New Mexico 97
☐ Thistle, Spiny Sow- 329
☐ Thistle, Yellow-spine 93
☐ Threefold, American 301
☐ Toadflax, Bastard 257
☐ Tobacco, Desert 215
☐ Turpentinebush 401
☐ Twinevine, Fringed 173
☐ Unicorn Plant, Desert 369
☐ Valerian, Arizona 107
☐ Verbena, Desert Sand 167
☐ Verbena, Goodding 165

☐ Verbena, MacDougal 177
☐ Vervain, Dakota Mock....155
☐ Violet, Canada 217
☐ Violet, Wanderer 135
☐ Wallflower, Western 399
☐ Wood Sorrel, Tenleaf........77
☐ Woolly Star, Miniature......21
☐ Yarrow, Common............269
☐ Yellowbells, Arizona 349
☐ Zinnia, Desert 229
☐ Zinnia, Plains..................335

ABOUT THE AUTHORS

Nora Mays Bowers

Nora Mays Bowers is a full-time writer and nature photographer. She earned a Master of Science degree in Ecology from the University of Arizona, writing her thesis and publishing several professional papers on Harris's Hawks. Nora received grants from the National Science Foundation, Sigma Xi, Arizona Wildlife Foundation and James R. Silliman Memorial Research Fund for her hawk research, as well as research awards from the American Ornithologists' Union and Western Bird Banding Association. A member of the North American Nature Photography Association and Canon Professional Services, Nora's photography credits include Birder's World Magazine, Ranger Rick and Arizona Wildlife Views, as well as images in many books and calendars. She is coauthor of *Cactus of Arizona Field Guide*, *Wildflowers of the Carolinas Field Guide* and *Kaufman Focus Guides: Mammals of North America*.

Rick Bowers

Rick Bowers is a nature photographer, naturalist and writer. He has been photographing wildlife and nature for more than 40 years. He received a Bachelor of Science degree in Wildlife Ecology from the University of Arizona. Before turning to professional photography and writing, he led nature tours for Victor Emanuel Nature Tours and his own tour company for 24 years. Rick led tours throughout the New World from Barrow, Alaska (the northernmost city in North America) to Tierra del Fuego (an island at the southern tip of South America) and Antarctica. He lived in Europe for six years as an Army "brat" and led tours in the Old World to the Kamchatka Peninsula of Siberia. Rick's photo credits span the gamut, from National Geographic and International Wildlife magazines to state and local fish and game publications. He is coauthor of *Cactus of Arizona Field Guide*, *Wildflowers of the Carolinas Field Guide* and *Kaufman Focus Guides: Mammals of North America*.

Rick and Nora live in Tucson, Arizona, with their cat, Beau, Dreamer the horse, and their donkey, Buddy. They can be reached through their web page at www.bowersphoto.com.

STAN TEKIELA

Naturalist, wildlife photographer and writer Stan Tekiela is the originator of the popular *Birds of Arizona Field Guide*. Stan has authored more than 190 educational books, including field guides, quick guides, nature books, children's books, playing cards and more, presenting many species of animals and plants.

With a Bachelor of Science degree in Natural History from the University of Minnesota and as an active professional naturalist for more than 30 years, Stan studies and photographs wildlife throughout the United States and Canada. He has received various national and regional awards for his books and photographs. Also a well-known columnist and radio personality, his syndicated column appears in more than 25 newspapers, and his wildlife programs are broadcast on a number of Midwest radio stations. Stan can be followed on Facebook and Twitter. He can be contacted via www.naturesmart.com.